中国民俗与民间艺术
Chinese Folklore and Folk Art

[美]王双双　编著

图书在版编目（CIP）数据

中国民俗与民间艺术/（美）王双双编著. —北京：北京大学出版社，2021.6
新双双中文教材
ISBN 978-7-301-32188-1

Ⅰ.①中… Ⅱ.①王… Ⅲ.①汉语—对外汉语教学—教材 ②风俗习惯—介绍—中国 ③民间艺术—介绍—中国 Ⅳ.①H195.4 ②K892 ③J12

中国版本图书馆CIP数据核字（2021）第094243号

书　　　名	中国民俗与民间艺术 ZHONGGUO MINSU YU MINJIAN YISHU
著作责任者	［美］王双双　编著
英文翻译	张瓅月
责任编辑	邓晓霞
标准书号	ISBN 978-7-301-32188-1
出版发行	北京大学出版社
地　　　址	北京市海淀区成府路205号　100871
网　　　址	http://www.pup.cn　　新浪微博：@北京大学出版社
电子信箱	zpup@pup.cn
电　　　话	邮购部 010-62752015　发行部 010-62750672　编辑部 010-62753334
印刷者	北京宏伟双华印刷有限公司
经销者	新华书店 889毫米×1194毫米　16开本　12.25印张　236千字 2021年6月第1版　2022年9月第2次印刷
定　　　价	98.00元（含课本、练习本、音频）

未经许可，不得以任何方式复制或抄袭本书之部分或全部内容。
版权所有，侵权必究
举报电话：010-62752024　电子信箱：fd@pup.pku.edu.cn
图书如有印装质量问题，请与出版部联系，电话：010-62756370

第二版序

能够与北京大学出版社合作出版"双双中文教材"的第二版，让这套优秀的对外汉语教材泽被更多的学生，加州中文教学研究中心倍感荣幸。

这是一套洋溢着浓浓爱意的教材。作者的女儿在美国出生，到了识字年龄，作者教她学习过市面上流行的多套中文教材，但都强烈地感觉到这些教材"水土不服"。一解女儿学习中文的燃眉之急，是作者编写这套教材的初衷和原动力。为了让没有中文环境的孩子能够喜欢学习中文，作者字斟句酌地编写课文；为了赋予孩子审美享受、引起他们的共鸣，作者特邀善画儿童创作了一幅幅稚气可爱的插图；为了加深孩子们对内容的理解，激发孩子们的学习热情，作者精心设计了充满创造性的互动活动。

这是一套承载着文化传承使命感的教材。语言不仅仅是文化的载体，更是文化重要的有机组成部分。学习一门外语的深层障碍往往根植于目标语言与母语间的文化差异。这种差异对于学习中文的西方学生尤为突出。这套教材的使用对象正处在好奇心和好胜心最强的年龄阶段，作者抓住了这一特点，变阻力为动力，一改过去削学生认知能力和智力水平之"足"以适词汇和语言知识之"履"的通病。教材在高年级部分，一个学期一个文化主题，以对博大精深的中国文化的探索激发学生的学习兴趣，使学生在学习语言的同时了解璀璨的中国文化。

"双双中文教材"自2005年面世以来，受到了老师、学生和家长的广泛欢迎。很多觉得中文学习枯燥无味而放弃的学生，因这套教材发现了学习中文的乐趣，又重新回到了中文课堂。本次修订，作者不仅吸纳了老师们对于初版的反馈意见和自己实际使用过程中的心得，还参考了近年对外汉语教学理论及实践方面的成果。语言学习部分由原来的九册改为五册，一学年学习一册，文化学习部分保持一个专题一册。相信修订后的"新双双中文教材"会更方便、实用，让更多学生受益。

张晓江
美国加州中文教学研究中心秘书长

第一版前言

"双双中文教材"是一套专门为海外青少年编写的中文课本,是我在美国八年的中文教学实践基础上编写成的。在介绍这套教材之前,请读一首小诗:

> 一双神奇的手,
> 推开一扇窗。
> 一条神奇的路,
> 通向灿烂的中华文化。
>
> 鲍凯文　鲍维江

鲍维江和鲍凯文姐弟俩是美国生美国长的孩子,也是我的学生。1998年冬,他们送给我的新年贺卡上的小诗,深深地打动了我的心。我把这首诗看成我文化教学的"回声"。我要传达给海外每位中文老师:我教给他们(学生)中国文化,他们思考了、接受了、回应了。这条路走通了!

语言是一种交流的工具,更是一种文化和一种生活方式,所以学习中文也就离不开中华文化的学习。汉字是一种古老的象形文字,她从远古走来,带有大量的文化信息,但学起来并不容易。使学生增强兴趣、减小难度,走出苦学汉字的怪圈,走进领悟中华文化的花园,是我编写这套教材的初衷。

学生不论大小,天生都有求知的欲望,都有欣赏文化美的追求。中华文化本身是魅力十足的。把这宏大而玄妙的文化,深入浅出地,有声有色地介绍出来,让这迷人的文化如涓涓细流,一点一滴地渗入学生们的心田,使学生们逐步体味中国文化,是我编写这套教材的目的。

为此我将汉字的学习放入文化介绍的流程之中同步进行,让同学们在学中国地理的同时,学习汉字;在学中国历史的同时,学习汉字;在学中国哲学的同时,学习汉字;在学中国科普文选的同时,学习汉字……

这样的一种中文学习,知识性强,趣味性强;老师易教,学生易学。当学生们合上书本时,他们的眼前是中国的大好河山,是中国五千年的历史和妙不可言的哲学思维,是奔腾的现代中国……

总之,他们了解了中华文化,就会探索这片土地,热爱这片土地,就会与中国结下情缘。

最后我要衷心地感谢所有热情支持和帮助我编写教材的老师、家长、学生、朋友和家人。特别是老同学唐玲教授、何茜老师和我女儿Uta Guo年复一年的鼎力相助。可以说这套教材是大家努力的结果。

王双双

课程设置（建议）

序号	书名	适用年级
1	中文课本　第一册	幼儿园/一年级
2	中文课本　第二册	二年级
3	中文课本　第三册	三年级
4	中文课本　第四册	四年级
5	中文课本　第五册	五年级
6	中国成语故事	六年级
7	中国地理常识	六年级
8	中国古代故事	七年级
9	中国神话传说	七年级
10	中国古代科学技术	八年级
11	中国民俗与民间艺术	八年级
12	中国文学欣赏	九年级
13	中国诗歌欣赏	九年级
14	中国古代哲学	十年级
15	中国历史	十年级

目录

第一课　二十四节气 …………………………… 1

第二课　喜庆的节日 …………………………… 16

第三课　独特的民居 …………………………… 29

第四课　中国古建筑 …………………………… 41

第五课　京剧 …………………………………… 54

第六课　茶 ……………………………………… 64

第七课　中国菜 ………………………………… 78

第八课　书法艺术 ……………………………… 89

第九课　中国武术 ……………………………… 101

第十课　民间艺术——剪纸 …………………… 112

生字表（简） …………………………………… 123

生字表（繁） …………………………………… 125

生词表（简） …………………………………… 127

生词表（繁） …………………………………… 129

附录　"新双双中文教材"写作练习（1—11册）… 131

第一课

二十四节气

姐姐上小学一年级时,老师就教了一首《二十四节气歌》。老师说:"在中国,民俗中的节气很重要,中国人的生活,衣、食、住、行,从来就没有离开过二十四节气。读懂二十四节气,就能聆听自然的声音。"

二十四节气是中国特有的。它产生于黄河中下游地区。中国先民通过对大自然的长期观察,根据太阳的活动,把一年分成24份,每份是一个节气,用来表示季节、气候和物候的变化。这样差不多每15天就是一个节气。节气在公历中,日期为:上半年的6日和21日前后;下半年的8日和23日前后。*让我们先学学《二十四节气歌》。

金山农民画

二十四节气歌

春雨惊春清谷天,
夏满芒(máng)夏暑相连。
秋处露秋寒霜降,
冬雪雪冬小大寒。

---

*上半年指1-6月,下半年指7-12月。

中国民俗与民间艺术

那么二十四节气的名称是什么呢？它们是：

立春	雨水	惊蛰(jīng zhé)	春分	清明	谷雨
立夏	小满	芒种(máng zhòng)	夏至	小暑	大暑
立秋	处暑	白露	秋分	寒露	霜降
立冬	小雪	大雪	冬至	小寒	大寒

节气的名字很有趣，两个字就说出了节气的特点。

比如：立春，"立"意为开始，春季开始了。

雨水，开始下雨，不再下雪了。

惊蛰，"蛰"意为藏，春雷响，惊醒了冬眠的虫子。

春分，"分"意为平分。这天，白天和黑夜一样长。

大暑，一年中最热的时候。

大寒，一年中最冷的时候。

那二十四节气如何影响人们的生活呢？让我们慢慢了解。

阮思齐（12岁） 画

（一）节气与农事安排

俗话说"民以食为天"，中国古来是一个农耕国家，种地打粮食是重中之重。而节气呢，除了告诉人们天气冷暖的变化，还与安排农事息息相关。在中国，节气农谚不在少数，比如：

"清明前后，种瓜点豆。"

"多插立夏yāng秧，稻谷收满仓。"

它提醒农民不误农时地进行春耕、夏耘、秋收、冬藏。节气农谚口耳相传，千百年来是农家人人都会的口诀。

金山农民画

（二）节气与传统节日

清明是一个节气，也是中国的一个重要传统节日：清明节（公历4月5日前后）。清明时节，正是春天，天清气朗，草木新生。清明节，人们扫墓祭祖，表达对亲人与祖先的怀念。

阮思齐（12岁） 画

（三）节气与饮食

立春是二十四节气中的第一个，这天，人们要吃春饼，迎接春天的到来。

谷雨，南方开始采茶，谷雨这天总要喝点儿新茶。

夏至，许多地方有吃面的习惯。这时天气炎热，把凉面用酱和黄瓜丝、豆芽等拌在一起，很可口。

谷雨采新茶

冬至，这天吃饺子。有"冬至饺子夏至面"之说。

还有"小雪腌菜，大雪腌(yān)肉"等许多与节气有关的制作食品的习俗。

春饼

凉面

（四）节气与诗歌

节气在变换，自然风景也在变换，从古至今，有许多描写节气的诗歌，如唐朝杜牧的诗《清明》：

清明时节雨纷纷，

路上行人欲断魂。

借问酒家何处有？

牧童遥指杏花村。

清明

节气之妙，是说不完的话题。几千年来，二十四节气在中国家喻户晓，现在已成为世界非物质文化遗产了。

生词

jié qì 节气	solar terms		lǎng 朗	bright
mín sú 民俗	folklore		sǎo mù 扫墓	sweep a grave
líng tīng 聆听	listen carefully		jì zǔ 祭祖	offer sacrifices to ancestors
shǔ 暑	summer heat		yǐn shí 饮食	diet
shuāng 霜	frost		jiàng 酱	sauce
liáng shi 粮食	food		bàn 拌	mix
nóng yàn 农谚	farmers' saying		xí sú 习俗	custom
yún 耘	cultivation		hún 魂	soul
kǒu jué 口诀	formula		mù tóng 牧童	shepherd boy
chuán tǒng 传统	traditional		yí chǎn 遗产	heritage

听写

节气　民俗　暑　霜　粮食　口诀　传统　朗

饮食　酱　拌　习俗　遗产　*扫墓　牧童

比一比

俗 { 俗话 / 习俗 / 民俗

酱 { 果子酱 / 酱油 / 酱菜

绊　拌　　祭　蔡

{ 绊倒 / 凉拌菜

{ 祭祖 / 蔡伦

词语运用

息息相关

① 水与人民生活息息相关。

② 二十四节气与农民安排农事息息相关。

③ 森林的保护与森林中的动物息息相关。

家喻户晓

① 孙悟空是家喻户晓的神话人物。

② 小说《三国演义》中的诸葛亮，在中国家喻户晓。

③ 他已成为家喻户晓的电影明星。

词语解释

物候——动植物的生长、发育、活动的规律。

农事——指耕地、播种、除草、防病虫害、收割等农业活动。

息息相关——彼此呼吸都相互关联，形容关系非常密切。

家喻户晓——家家户户都知道。

安排——处理（事情）。

思考题

节气与日历有什么不同？（参看11页资料）

日 历	节 气
标有年、月、日、星期、节日，有的或加有节气	节气不是日历
一般与安排农事无关	与安排农事相关，有些节气也是节日

阅读

二十四节气农事歌

春

立春天气暖，
雨水肥送完。
惊蛰快耙(bà)地，
春分犁(lí)不闲。
清明多栽树，
谷雨要种田。

夏

立夏点瓜豆，
小满不种棉。
芒种收新麦，
夏至快犁田。
小暑不算热，
大暑是伏(fú)天。

秋

立秋种白菜，
处暑摘新棉。
白露要打枣，
秋分种麦田。
寒露收割完，
霜降把地翻。

冬

立冬收完菜，
小雪犁耙开。
大雪天已冷，
冬至换长天。
小寒快买办，
大寒过新年。

小满蚕节

小满是节气,也是一个节日。相传这天是蚕神的生日,所以江浙一带有祭蚕神的习俗。小满时节,蚕宝宝长大吐丝,蚕农会将新丝拿到集市上卖。

祭蚕

资料

日	一	二	三	四	五	六
			1 元旦节	2 腊八节	3 初九	4 初十
5 十一	6 小寒	7 十三	8 十四	9 十五	10 十六	11 十七
12 十八	13 十九	14 二十	15 廿一	16 廿二	17 小年	18 廿四
19 廿五	20 大寒	21 廿七	22 廿八	23 廿九	24 除夕	25 春节
26 初二	27 初三	28 初四	29 初五	30 初六	31 初七	

公历 2020 年 1 月 农历庚子年【鼠年】

中国日历（标有公历/农历年、月、日、星期、节日、二十四节气）

二十四节气图表

Lesson One

Twenty-Four Solar Terms

When my sister was in first grade, her teacher taught her *The Song of Twenty-Four Solar Terms*. "Solar terms are very important in Chinese folklore. Chinese people live their lives in close connection with the twenty-four solar terms—they dress, eat, live, and move about accordingly. If one understands the twenty-four solar terms, one can hear the sound of mother nature." said the teacher.

The twenty-four solar terms are unique to Chinese. The terms came into being in the midstream and downstream regions of Yellow River. Through long-term observation of nature, Chinese ancestors divided one year into 24 equal parts based on the solar movements. Each part is a solar term used to represent the changes of season, climate, and phenology. This makes approximately every 15 days a solar term. In the Gregorian calendar, the solar terms are around the 6th and 21st of each month in the first half of the year, around the 8th and 23rd of each month in the second half of the year. Let's learn *The Song of Twenty-Four Solar Terms*.

The Song of Twenty-Four Solar Terms

Spring begins, Rain Water awaken insects; after Spring Equinox is Pure Brightness and then Grain Rain;

Summer starts Grain Buds and Grain in Ear; then the Summer Solstice, the Slight and Great Heat come along.

Autumn stops the heat, White Dew descends, then after Autumn Equinox, Cold Dew and cold frost fall down;

Winter comes with Slight and Great Snow; after the Winter Solstice, the Slight and Great Cold are around.

Then what are the names of twenty-four solar terms? They are:

Lichun(Start of Spring), Yushui (Rain Water), Jingzhe (Waking of Insects), Chunfen (Spring Equinox), Qingming (Pure Brightness), Guyu (Grain Rain),

Lixia (Start of Summer), Xiaoman (Grain Buds), Mangzhong (Grain in Ear), Xiazhi (Summer Solstice), Xiaoshu (Slight Heat), Dashu (Great Heat),

Liqiu (Start of Autumn), Chushu (End of Heat), Bailu (White Dew), Qiufen (Autumn Equinox), Hanlu (Cold Dew), Shuangjiang (Frost Descent),

Lidong (Start of Winter), Xiaoxue (Slight Snow), Daxue (Great Snow), Dongzhi (Winter Solstice), Xiaohan (Slight Cold), Dahan (Great Cold).

The names of solar terms are very interesting as each term uses two Chinese characters to tell the characteristics of the term.

Look at the examples:

Lichun, (Start of Spring): Li means to begin; spring begins.

Yushui (Rain Water): The rain falls down; it doesn't snow anymore.

Jingzhe (Waking of Insects): Zhe means to hide. Spring thunder rolls, awakening the hibernating insects.

Chunfen (Spring Equinox): Fen means to divide equally. On this day, day time and night time are equally long.

Dashu (Great Heat): The hottest time of a year.

Dahan (Great Cold): The coldest time of a year.

So how do the twenty-four solar terms affect people's life? Let us learn it little by little.

1. Solar Terms and Agricultural Arrangements

The old saying goes that "Food is everything to the people". China has been an agricultural country since the ancient times; therefore, farming and harvesting are the topmost priorities. Solar terms not only alert people of climate changes; they are also closely related to agricultural arrangements. In China, there are quite a few agricultural proverbs that help farmers plan their spring plowing, summer cultivation, autumn harvest, and winter storage. For examples, "Around Pure Brightness, plant melons and beans." "Plant more Start of Summer rice shoots to fill the rice bins." Proverbs about agriculture-related solar terms are passed on among farmers by word of mouth for thousands of years.

2. Solar Terms and Traditional Festivals

Qingming, "Pure Brightness", (around Gregorian calendar Apr. 5th) is a solar term and a very important traditional festival in China. The name of Qingming Festival is related to the characteristics of weather and phenology at that time. At this time of the year, the sky is bright, the air is clear, grasses are green, and spring is everywhere. For this festival, people visit the graves of their ancestors and make offerings to them, remembering their deceased family members and ancestors with love and respect.

3. Solar Terms and Food

Lichun (Start of Spring), is the first of the twenty-four solar terms. On this day, people eat Spring pancakes to welcome the arrival of spring. Guyu (Grain Rain) starts the event of tea leaf picking in the South. On this day, people drink fresh tea made in the same year. On Xiazhi (Summer Solstice), there is the habit of eating noodles in many places. Being hot at this time of the year, it's a real pleasure to eat delicious cold noodles mixed with sauce paste and raw fresh vegetables such as shredded cucumber

and bean sprouts. On Dongzhi (Winter solstice)", people eat dumplings. There is a saying of, "Dumplings for Dongzhi, noodles for Xiazhi". Another saying goes "Marinate vegetables on Xiaoxue (Slight Snow); marinate meat on Daxue (Great Snow)." There are many folk customs of preparing food according to solar terms.

4. Solar Terms and Poetry

The change of solar terms brings about changing natural scenes. Ever since the ancient times, there have been many beautiful poems describing solar terms. For example, the Tang Dynasty poet Du Mu wrote about Qingming in the poem below:

Qingming (Pure Brightness)

It drizzles endlessly on the Qingming (Pure Brightness) day,

Travelers are heart-broken along their way.

When I asked "where can I find a winehouse?"

The shepherd boy pointed at a village afar among the apricot flowers.

There is no end to the wonders of solar terms. For thousands of years, the twenty-four solar terms are known in all households. Now the twenty-four solar terms have become a world intangible cultural heritage.

Songs of Agricultural Activity Related to the Twenty-Four Solar Terms

Spring

With Start of Spring days become warm.

Every farmer in his land begins to toil.

By Rain Water they must finish fertilizing the soil.

On Waking of Insects they are busy harrowing.

On Spring Equinox, they cannot idle but must be ploughing.

On Pure Brightness they plant many trees.

On Grain Rain they plant the seeds.

Summer

On Start of Summer, sow the seeds of melons and beans,

On Grain Buds, don't plant the cotton.

On Grain in Ear, harvest the new wheat,

On Summer Solstice, hurry to plow the land.

Slight Heat is not real hot,

Great Heat is the hottest day.

Autumn

On Start of Autumn, plant cabbages,

On End of Heat, pick the new cotton.
On White Dew, harvest dates with sticks.
On Autumn Equinox, plant wheats in the land.
On Cold Dew, finish harvesting,
On Frost Descent, plough the land.

Winter

On Start of Winter, finish harvesting the vegetables,
On Slight Snow, rake the land with the plow.
On Great Snow, the day is cold,
On Winter Solstice, the day time becomes longer.
On Slight Cold, hurry to buy festival goods,
On Great Cold, begin to celebrate the New Year.

Xiaoman Silkworm Festival

Xiaoman(Grain Buds) is a solar term, and also a festival. The legend goes that this day is the birthday of the Silkworm Goddess. In areas of Jiangsu and Zhejiang there is the custom of making offering to the Silkworm Goddess. Around Xiaoman, the silkworms grow big enough to produce thread. Silkworm raisers will go to the market to sell the newly made silk.

第二课

喜庆的节日

春节是中国农历新年,是中国人心中最重要的节日。看,春节前的火车站、汽车站、飞机场都挤满了回家的人。回家!回家!回家!无论多大的风雪,也挡不住人们回家的脚步。

春节在中国农历的正月初一(公历1月底2月初),正是冬末春初,所以叫春节。过年前,无论城市还是农村,到处都是浓浓的节日气氛:街旁的树上挂着一串串红灯笼,商店里堆满了各种年货;家家户户的大门上贴上了大红春联;房屋清扫得干干净净;人们在窗户上贴窗花,往墙上贴年画;妈妈做好了各种食品:糖果、糕点……准备过年了!

春节

按中国的习俗，春节是团圆的日子。人们从四面八方赶回家中与亲人团聚。俗话说："一年不赶，赶三十晚！"意思是一定要春节前赶回家过年。那是人们期盼的幸福时光：一年一次的全家大团圆。爷爷奶奶，爸爸妈妈，儿子女儿，都放下了手中的工作和学习，在一起过大年。

俗话说："有钱没钱，吃饺子过年。"这是说过年一定要吃饺子的。那什么时候吃饺子呢？春节的前夜叫"除夕"。除夕之夜，家人围坐在一起吃年夜饭，聊天说笑，看电视里的春晚节目，乐融融，喜洋洋，直到天明。除夕零点的钟声一响，人们就吃饺子，意思是"更岁交子"，吃过饺子就算过了年了。

过了除夕就是大年初一，人们纷纷走亲戚、看朋友，互相拜年，见面时常说"恭喜发财""健康长寿"等吉祥祝福的话。孩子们给老人拜年，会拿到一个红包。

过年，最快活的要数孩子们。他们穿上新衣服，和小伙伴们一起放烟花和爆竹，看舞龙舞狮的游行表演，品尝街上的小吃……哪儿都是欢天喜地快乐的人群。

在喜庆的春节里，我们看到最多的颜色是红色：红灯笼、红春联、红剪纸、红包……在中国文化中，"红"是火的颜色，代表生活红红火火，越来越富裕。

春节到，春节到，
穿新衣，戴新帽。
贴春联，挂红灯，
舞龙舞狮放鞭炮。
全家团圆吃饺子，
拜年得个大红包！

第二课

生词

xǐ qìng 喜庆	joyful	qīn qi 亲戚	relatives
jǐ mǎn 挤满	crowded	bài nián 拜年	Happy New Year
nóng 浓	thick, strong	gōng xǐ 恭喜	congratulate
qì fēn 气氛	atmosphere	jí xiáng 吉祥	good luck
tiē 贴	stick	zhù fú 祝福	bless
tuán jù 团聚	reunion	yóu xíng 游行	parade
jiǎo zi 饺子	dumplings	jiǎn 剪	cut
chú xī 除夕	Chinese New Year's Eve	fù yù 富裕	rich
liáo tiān 聊天	chat	biān pào 鞭炮	firecrackers

听写

喜庆　挤满　气氛　贴　团聚　饺子　聊天

亲戚　祝福　游行　剪　富裕　*拜年

比一比

$\begin{cases}喜庆\\庆祝\end{cases}$ $\begin{cases}团聚\\团圆\end{cases}$ $\begin{cases}游行\\旅游\end{cases}$

近义词

期盼——盼望　　　　祝福——祝愿

反义词

喜庆——悲伤　　贴——揭　　浓——淡

学说吉祥话

恭喜发财

心想事成

万事如意

美梦成真

词语运用

恭喜

① 恭喜你，考上了理想的大学。

② 恭喜你，当了爸爸！

③ 恭喜你，当了飞行员！

祝

① 祝春节快乐！

② 祝你生日快乐！

③ 祝爷爷奶奶健康长寿！

④ 祝你成功！

词语解释

年货——春节时买的吃的、穿的、用的、玩的、礼品等统称年货。

春联——过年时贴在门两侧，写有喜庆文字的红纸，表达美好愿望。

乐融融——快乐和睦(mù)的样子。

春晚——春节联欢晚会。

红包——过年长辈给孩子们的压岁钱放在红色纸袋里，叫红包。

中国民俗与民间艺术

阅读

元宵节
（xiāo）

春节过后两周，又一个喜庆节日"元宵节"来了。

元宵节在农历正月十五。这天晚上，人们会去观赏花灯。花灯五光十色，有宫灯、花卉灯、人物灯、动物灯、玩具灯……一片灯的海洋。有的花灯上还写着灯谜，比如"千条线，万条线，掉到河里看不见"就是一个灯谜，能猜出来吗？

元宵节，吃元宵是不能少的。元宵是用糯米粉做的小圆球，里面包着糖和果仁，味道香甜可口。

元宵花灯

吃元宵

刘滢（7岁） 画

元宵猜灯谜

22

端午节

农历五月初五是端午节。这个节日是为了纪念中国古代伟大的诗人屈原。屈原是战国时期楚国人,是楚国的高官,主张联合其他诸侯国共同抵抗(dǐ kàng)秦国。楚王不听,还把他赶出国都。后来楚国被秦国打败,屈(qū)原非常悲痛,跳江自杀了。人们听到屈原跳江的消息,急忙划船去打捞他的尸体,但是没有找到。为了不让鱼儿吃掉屈原的身体,百姓们就把食物扔进江里喂鱼。后来形成了五月初五,人们吃粽(zòng)子、赛龙船的习俗。

粽子

端午节划龙舟

中秋节

农历八月十五是中秋节。八月是秋天,十五又是八月中间的一天,所以这个节叫中秋节。

秋季,天气晴朗,天上很少有浮云,月亮也显得很明亮。秋天,瓜果熟了,粮食收了。中秋节的晚上,全家人坐在一起,摆上水果和月饼,一边赏月,一边品尝月饼。月饼是圆的,意思是团圆。月饼有很多品种:甜的、咸的、肉的、蛋黄的。月饼上还有花纹和字样,又好吃又好看。

"月亮上有什么?"弟弟问。奶奶说:"月亮上有美丽的嫦娥、捣药的玉兔,还有一棵桂花树和一个不停地砍桂树的人——吴刚。"

中秋节,家人团聚,那些远离故乡的人,会在同一个夜晚,望着明月思念家乡,思念亲人。

中秋赏月

月饼

资料

中国主要节日

节日名称	节日时间	节日内容
春节	农历正月初一	贴春联　挂红灯　吃饺子　做年糕　穿新衣　放鞭炮　舞龙舞狮　拜年　红包
元宵节	农历正月十五	赏花灯　猜灯谜　吃元宵
端午节	农历五月初五	纪念爱国诗人屈原　吃粽子　赛龙舟
中秋节	农历八月十五	家人团聚　赏月　吃月饼　嫦娥的故事

口语练习

在熟悉课文的基础上，口头讲述中国的节日（春节、元宵节、端午节、中秋节）。

Lesson Two

The Joyful Festival

Spring Festival, the Chinese New Year in lunar calendar, is the most important festival in all Chinese people's hearts. Look! All the train stations, bus terminals, and airports before the Spring Festival are crowded with people eagering to return home. Go home! Go Home! Go back Home! No matter how heavy the snowstorm may be, it cannot stop people from going home.

Spring Festival is the first day of the first month in Chinese lunar calendar (at the end of January or the beginning of February in Gregorian calendar). As it falls at the end of winter and the start of spring, it is called the Spring Festival. Before the festival, whether in the city or countryside, the festive spirit permeates the air. Strings of red lanterns hang from trees along the street; shops are filled with all kinds of goods for the festival. Doors of every household are decorated with red spring couplets; all rooms are swept and cleaned. People put paper flowers on the windows and New Year's pictures on the walls, and moms make all kinds of food, like candies and cakes. Ready for the Chinese New Year!

According to the ancient customs in China, Spring Festival is the day for family reunion. People from everywhere rush home to get together with their families. As the old saying goes, "No rush in the whole year except on the New Year's Eve!" It means one must return home to celebrate the New Year with family before the Spring Festival. It's the happy moment all families long for: the family reunion once in a year. Grandpas and grandmas, dads and moms, sons and daughters, they all stop their work or study, get together and celebrate the New Year.

The old saying says "Rich or poor, eat dumplings for the New Year", meaning New Year is not celebrated without eating dumplings. Then when should dumplings be eaten? The night before Spring Festival is called New Year's Eve. On that night, the whole family sits around to enjoy the New Year feast, chatting with each other, playing jokes and laughing together, watching the Spring Festival Gala on TV, happy and joyous until dawn. As soon as the midnight clock strikes on New Year's Eve, people begin to eat dumplings. It means "the time changes in the Zi hour and the old year is taken over by the new year". After eating dumplings, the New Year celebration is done.

After the New Year's Eve is the first day of New Year. People on this day visit relatives and friends, wishing each other Happy New Year. When they meet, they greet each other with auspicious blessings such as "Congratulations on your good fortune" "Wish you good health and long life". When kids pay a new year's call to the seniors, they will get a red envelope with money inside.

The happiest people to celebrate the Chinese New Year are the kids. They put on new clothing, set off fireworks and firecrackers with their friends, watch the parade of dragon and lion dances, and enjoy street food—everywhere is crowded with joyous people.

The most common color we see during the festive Spring Festival is red: red lanterns, red Spring

Festival couplets, red paper cuttings, red envelopes—in Chinese culture red is the color of fire, representing prosperity and growing wealth.

The Lantern Festival

Two weeks after the Spring Festival, comes another joyful festival, the Lantern Festival.

The Lantern Festival falls on the fifteenth day of the first Lunar month. In the evening of this day, people will go out to watch the colorful lanterns which are splendid in all beautiful colors, with all kinds of designs such as palaces, flowers, human characters, animal forms, toys and etc., forming a sea of lights.

On some colorful lanterns there are lantern riddles. For example, "One thousand lines, ten thousand lines, all fall into the river and none finds" is a riddle. Can you guess what it is?

On Lantern Festival, eating Yuanxiao is indispensable. Yuanxiao are small round balls made of sticky rice flour with sugar and nuts as fillings, tasting sweet and delicious.

The Dragon Boat Festival

On the fifth day of the fifth month of the lunar calendar is the Dragon Boat Festival.

This festival is to commemorate the great ancient Chinese poet Qu Yuan. A citizen and once a senior official in the State of Chu in the period of Warring States, Qu Yuan advocated allying with other states to fence off the state of Qin. However, the king of Chu didn't listen to him and banished him away from the capital. Later Chu was defeated by Qin. Qu Yuan was devastated and committed suicide by jumping into a river. On hearing about the news of his death, people hurried to search for his body in boats but couldn't find him. In order that the fish didn't eat Qu Yuan's body, people threw food into the river to feed the fish. From then on it has formed the tradition of eating Zongzi (steamed sticky rice wrapped in plant leaves) and holding dragon boat racing on the fifth day of the fifth lunar month.

The Mid-Autumn Festival

The fifteenth day of the eighth month in lunar calendar is the Mid-Autumn Festival. The eighth lunar month is in the autumn; the fifteenth day sits in the middle of the month, so the festival is called Mid-Autumn Festival.

In autumn, the weather is clear and sunny. During the day there is scarcely any cloud; in the night the moon also seems very bright. In autumn, melons and vegetables are ripe; the grains are harvested. On the night of Mid-Autumn Festival, the whole family sit together around a table with fruits and moon-cakes on it, enjoying the moon and tasting the cakes. The moon-cakes are round, meaning togetherness and unity. There are all kinds of moon-cakes: sweet ones, salty ones, containing meat or egg yolks fillings. There are also decorations of pattern and characters on the outside of the moon-cakes, making the cakes beautiful and tasty.

"What is there in the moon?" Little brother asks.

"In the moon there is a beautiful goddess named Chang'e, a white rabbit making medicines, an osmanthus tree, and a person named Wu Gang who chops the tree non-stop." Answers Granny.

On the Mid-Autumn Festival, all family members get together for the reunion. Those who are far away from hometown, will on the same night, look at the bright moon, think of their home and their beloved people.

第三课

独特的民居

（一）四合院

在北京老城区胡同里行走，常看到红门灰瓦的四合院，很是优雅。春天，院墙上挂满紫藤(téng)花，可是大门却紧闭，让人总想看看里面神秘的院落。

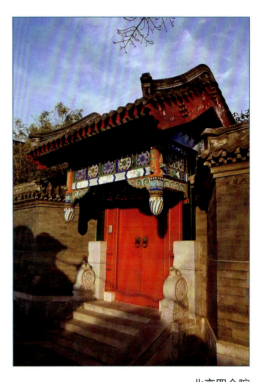

北京四合院

四合院是汉族的传统民居，其中北京四合院最有代表性。它是一种四面房子围起来的院落。北面是正房，东西是厢房，南面是客房，中间是庭院，关了院门，就是一个封闭的空间。院落里居住着一大家人：长辈住正房，晚辈住厢房，尊老爱幼，相互照顾。院子里会种树，种花，养鱼。人们春天看花，夏天乘凉，秋天吃果子，冬天赏雪，一年四季，无一日不好。四合院是一个安逸宁静的家园。

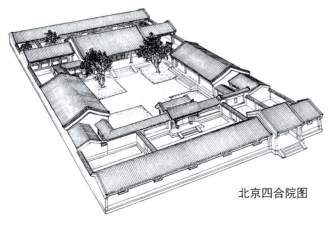

北京四合院图

（二）窑洞

在中国西北的黄土高原上，气候干燥少雨，黄土又细又黏(nián)，当地百姓创造了一种民居叫"窑洞"，它已有四千多年历史了。窑洞，一般是在黄土坡上直接往里挖洞。洞宽三四米，深七八米。洞顶为拱形，洞口安上门窗就成了一间住房。窑洞的好处是省工省料，住起来冬暖夏凉。当然窑洞因土中含有水汽，会比较潮湿。

选自《传家日历》（2018）

陕北窑洞

（三）江南民居

中国江南被称为水乡，水是南方民居独特的景致：民居多是前街后河。小河从门前屋后轻轻流过，取水方便，房屋也因水有了灵气。江南民居一般为二层，底层是砖结构，上层是木结构。外墙多用白色，还有高高的马头墙，又防火又美观。南方四季山清水秀，小桥流水，民居粉墙黛瓦，给人一种清新的感觉。

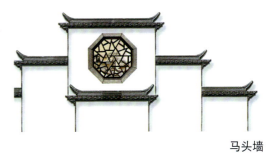

马头墙

江南民居

（四）蒙古包

在中国北部的大草原上，主要居住着蒙古族。他们放牧牛羊，为了水草常常搬家。所以他们的"住房"是一种容易搬动的"房子"，叫蒙古包。蒙古包是圆形的，一般面积不太大，直径4至6米，高2米，用木条搭成框架，外边再包上羊毛毡子。蒙古包中间放一个炉子，烧水做饭，冬天可以取暖；四周常常挂着美丽的挂毯，使小小的蒙古包有了生活气息。蒙古包的顶部有圆形的天窗，用来采光和通风。

蒙古包

蓝天白云，草原牛羊，蒙古包三五成群，这就是牧民的生活画面。

内蒙古草原

第三课

生 词

mín jū 民居	local-style dwelling houses		ān yì 安逸	at ease
yōu yǎ 优雅	elegant		yáo dòng 窑洞	cave
xiāng fáng 厢房	wing room		líng qì 灵气	reiki
tíng yuàn 庭院	courtyard		fáng huǒ 防火	fire prevention
fēng bì 封闭	close		zhí jìng 直径	diameter
zhǎng bèi 长辈	elders, senior		kuàng jià 框架	framework
zhào gù 照顾	take care of		zhān 毡	felt
chéng liáng 乘凉	enjoy the cool		guà tǎn 挂毯	tapestry

听 写

民居　庭院　封闭　长辈　照顾　安逸　窑洞

灵气　防火　直径　框架　壁　*乘凉　毯

比一比

秘 { 神秘 / 秘密 }　　厢 { 车厢 / 厢房 }　　庭 { 家庭 / 庭院 }

反义词

独特——普通　　优雅——低俗　　神秘——公开

传统——新潮　　长辈——晚辈　　安逸——紧张

词语运用

传统

① 妈妈穿的衣服，式样很传统。

② 中国的传统是一家人围着桌子一起吃饭。

③ 学风自由是这所大学的优良传统。

气氛

① 春节时，家家挂红灯笼贴春联，到处是节日的气氛。

② 会谈是在友好的气氛中进行的。

③ 口试开始了，教室里的气氛紧张起来。

词语解释

独特——特别的，独一无二、与众不同的。

胡同——北京的小街道。

院落——院子。

代表性——典型的。

北京四合院

土楼

中国东南沿海福建广东等地，有一种独特的民居——土楼。土楼的规模很大，形状有方形的，也有圆形的。外面是高大的土墙，墙上开窗很少，像是一座堡垒。古代由于战乱，一些北方人南迁到福建、广东一带，被称为客家人。他们常常全族人建土楼居住在一起，防卫自保，同时也保留了南迁前的文化传统和习俗。土楼的墙很厚，十分坚固，有的土楼有房屋300多间，中间是公共活动的地方。土楼内有水井，有粮仓。这种民居如今成了中外闻名的住宅奇观了。

福建土楼

福建土楼院内

天井式窑洞

还有一种是天井式窑洞，就是在平地上往下挖一个深井，深七八米，宽15米，长方形。再在方井的四壁往里挖洞作住房。从井内到地面有阶梯。井底院子种树，种花，真是个"地下四合院"。

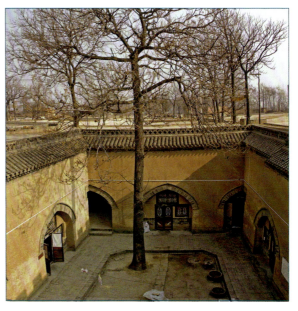

天井式窑洞

马头墙

江南民居的马头墙是指高于屋顶的墙。形状像马头，故称马头墙。马头墙是用砖砌成的，用于防火，也叫封火墙。就是这道为了安全的防火墙，也美得让人心动！

马头墙

Lesson Three

Unique Residential Buildings

1. Courtyard House

Walking through the Hutongs of the old city districts in Beijing, one often sees elegant red-door, grey-tiled courtyard houses. In spring, wisteria blossoms cover the walls of the courtyard, yet the gates are closed tight, making people wonder what's inside those mysterious courtyards.

Courtyard houses are residential buildings unique to the Han people. Beijing Courtyard house is the most representative. It is a courtyard enclosed by houses on the four sides. On the north is the main quarters, on the east and west side are the wings, to the south is the guest quarters, and in the middle is the courtyard. It's an enclosed space when the gate is closed. Inside it lives a big family: the older generation live in the main quarters, the younger generation in the wings; the young people respect the old, the old people love the young; everyone takes care of the others. Inside the courtyard, they plant trees and flowers, keep and breed fish. In spring, they watch the flowers; in summer, they enjoy the cool air; in autumn, they eat fruits; in winter, they enjoy the snow. In all seasons, not a single day is not enjoyable. The courtyard house is a peaceful and quiet home.

2. Yaodong

On the Loess Plateau in northwest China, where the climate is dry and rain is scarce and the loess is fine and sticky, the local people have created a type of dwelling called the "Yaodong"(cave dwelling) with a history of over 4,000 years. A Yaodong is usually a cave dug inside a loess slope, about 3 to 4 meters wide, 7 to 8 meters deep. The roof of the Yaodong is vaulted, and the entrance is fitted with doors and windows to form a dwelling. Yaodong has many advantages: it saves labor and materials; it's warm in winter and cool in summer. Of course, it is damp because of the moisture in the soil.

3. Jiangnan Residential Houses

Jiangnan (South of the Yangtze River) of China is known as water towns. Water is a unique feature of the southern dwellings: most of the houses face the street in the front and have the river running behind. The river flows gently in the front and back of the house, making it easy for people to fetch water, and gives the house a spiritual atmosphere. Jiangnan residential buildings are generally two-storied; the ground floor is paved with bricks and the upper floor paved with wood. Most of the

exterior walls are white and have high horse-head walls. These houses are both fireproof and beautiful. In all four seasons in the south, the mountains are green and the river water clear, small bridges go over the flowing water, residential houses with white walls and black tiles convey the simple elegance.

4. Mongolian Yurts

The vast grasslands of northern China are mainly inhabited by the Mongolian people, who often migrate for water and grass to herd cattle and sheep. So, their "residence" is a kind of easy-to-move "house", called "yurt". Yurts are round and small, 4 to 6 meters in diameter and 2 meters high, framed with wooden planks and wrapped with woolen blankets. A stove is put in the middle of the yurt to boil water and to cook, and heat the yurt up in winter. The walls around are often hung with beautiful felt carpets, making the small yurt full of warm atmosphere. There is a round skylight on the top of the yurt for natural lighting and better ventilation.

Blue sky, white clouds, endless grassland, cattle and sheep herds along the slopes, small groups close to each other—this is the picture of the herders' life.

Tulou (Earthen Building)

In areas of Fujian and Guangdong along the southeast coast of China, there is a unique kind of residence building—Tulou (the earthen building). The earthen building has a large size, in forms of square and circle. On the outside, there is a high earthen wall with very few windows, like a castle. In the old times, in order to escape from the wars, some Northern people moved southbound to the areas of Fujian and Guangdong and were called "Hakka people (visitor family clans)". The whole clan built and lived inside the earthen walls for defense and self-protection. They also kept their previous cultural traditions and customs formed before they moved to the south. The earthen building is very large, with very thick and solid walls outside, more than 300 houses inside, and a public place for activities in the middle. Inside the earthen building there are wells and barns. This kind of dwelling has now become a famous residential wonder in China and abroad.

Patio-Type Kiln

Another is the patio-type kiln, which is a deep rectangular well dug down on the flat ground, about seven or eight meters deep and 15 meters wide. Housing spaces are created by further digging into the earth from four sides of the square well. From the well there are stairs leading onto the ground. The courtyard at the bottom of the well is planted with trees and flowers, really an "underground courtyard".

Horse-Head Wall

The horse-head wall in residence dwellings is the wall higher than the roof, found in areas to the south of the Yangtze River. It is shaped like a horse's head, thus bearing the name of horse head wall. A horse head wall is made of bricks for fire prevention, also called fire sealing wall. This simple firewall for safety is also appealingly beautiful.

第四课

中国古建筑

中国有几千年的文明史，古代宫殿、寺庙等建筑都有鲜明的特点：木架结构和大屋顶。木架结构，就是先将地上的土夯(hāng)实，后在夯土上架木柱和梁，再加盖屋顶。

建筑的木架结构是由柱、梁、斗拱等组成的，其中斗拱是中国特有的结构，也是独有的构件，从艺术和技术两方面看，都可以说是中国古典建筑的精华。斗拱早在周代就出现了。斗拱由方形的斗和矩形的拱组成，斗——拱——斗……一层层叠加上去，形成上大下小的托架，能承重，支挑着"飞"出来的大屋檐。中国传统木结构建筑，构件之间不用钉子，而是用木头本身榫卯勾连在一起，有很强的抗震能力，有"墙倒屋不塌"的说法。如故宫的太和殿，屋顶重两千吨，就是靠木架斗拱托起的，经过了几百

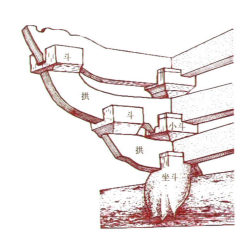

斗拱

北京故宫

年的风雨和地震，现在依然完好。

中国古建筑中的大屋顶最为精彩，在世界上也赢得了荣誉。想想看，原本巨大的宫殿四四方方坐落在高高的台基上，稳固庄严，正是大屋顶柔和的曲线，微翘的屋檐如鸟高飞，使宫殿端庄而优雅。大屋檐不仅美观，还可以让门窗和柱子防雨防潮。

现在世界上最大、保存最完好的古代木结构建筑群是北京的故宫。故宫，原名紫禁城，有六百多年的历史。故宫占地72万平方米，房屋九千余间，一片宫殿的海洋。宫殿的屋顶是金黄色的琉(liú)璃瓦，在阳光下闪闪发光。在金色屋檐下是蓝、绿、白三色彩绘，红色的立柱、门窗。大殿坐落在白色汉白玉台基上，金碧辉煌。

当我们学习中国古建筑时，不能忘记梁思成先生。他是中国古建筑研究的开创者，一生保护中国古建筑。他带领一个小组，十几年的时间，系统地考察了中国上千个古建筑，并精细测绘。之后，他写出了《中国建筑史》和英文版的《图像中国建筑史》，向中国和世

梁思成

界介绍中国古建筑的历史发展与辉煌成就。当人们看到他笔下的建筑图纸时，顿时心生敬意。图中融入了中国传统工笔白描的技巧，完美表现了中国古建筑独特的美感，每一笔都催人泪下。他在为古代工匠做记录，追回那将要湮没的古建筑艺术和技艺。

梁思成绘制的独乐寺观音阁剖面图

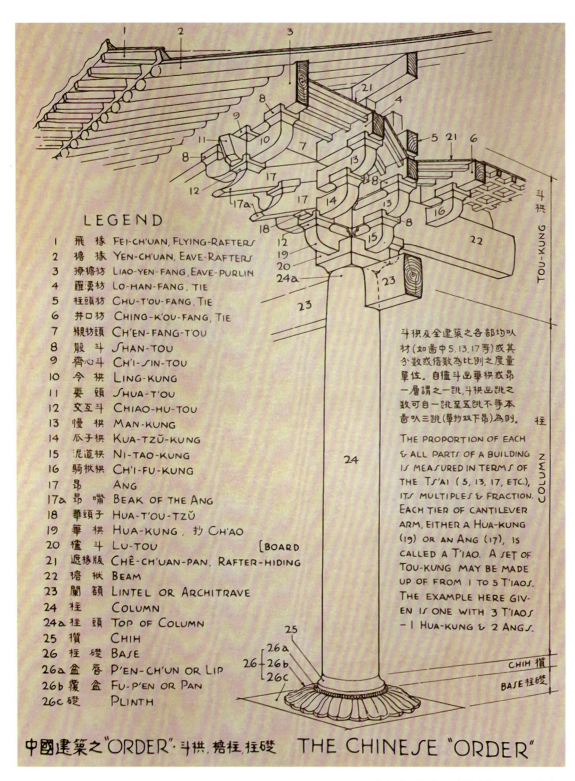

选自《图像中国建筑史》，梁思成绘制

第四课

生词

sì miào 寺庙	temple	róng yù 荣誉	honor
dǒu gǒng 斗拱	interlocking	wěn gù 稳固	solid
gòu jiàn 构件	wooden brackets constructional elements	zhuāng yán 庄严	solemn
		wēi qiào 微（翘）	curl up slightly
jǔ xíng 矩形	rectangle	zǐ jìn chéng 紫禁城	the Forbidden City
dié 叠	fold	jīn bì huī huáng 金碧辉煌	glittering
tuō 托	hold up	xì tǒng 系统	systematically; system
yán 檐	eave	cè huì 测绘	survey and draw
sǔn mǎo 榫卯	mortise and tenon	dùn shí 顿时	all at once
gōu lián 勾连	collude	bái miáo 白描	line drawing
dūn 吨	ton	yān mò 湮没	annihilate

听写

寺庙　斗拱　构件　矩形　托　勾连　吨　荣誉

稳固　庄严　系统　顿时　＊紫禁城　金碧辉煌

比一比

构 { 结构 / 构件 }　　防 { 防火 / 防雨 }

庄 { 村庄 / 庄严 }　　顿 { 顿时 / 一顿 }

禁 { 禁止 / 紫禁城 }　　禁止烟火　禁止停车

反义词

曲线——直线　　顿时——很久

近义词

顿时——马上、立刻　　禁止——不许、不准

词语运用

系统

① 他在大学时，就系统地学习了中国历史。

② 我把物理系统地复习了一遍，所以考试成绩很好。

③ 胃病是消化系统的病。

顿时

① 明星歌手一上台，台下顿时欢声雷动。

② 这道数学题让他一讲，我顿时就明白了。

③ 老师说今天不考试，大家心情顿时就放松了。

词语解释

精华——事物最好的部分。

台基——建筑的基础。

开创者——开拓一个新领域、建设一个新事物的第一人。

成就——成绩，业绩。

技艺——技术工艺。

梁思成与佛光寺

梁思成（1901—1972），中国著名建筑学家，中国古建筑研究的开创者。他早年在美国宾(bīn)夕法尼亚大学学习建筑学，发现中国这个文明古国竟然没有中国人自己写的建筑史，于是他立志写一部《中国建筑史》。那时有日本学者认为，中国已不存在唐代木结构建筑了。

从1931年起，梁思成带领一个小组，考察了中国二百多个市、县的上千个古建筑，并对其中的大多数进行精细的测绘。幸运的是，1937年梁思成在敦(dūn)煌唐代壁画《五台山图》中发现了佛光寺。他非常兴奋，确信中国还有唐代木结构建筑。于是他和夫

山西五台县佛光寺

人林徽因及助手动身去山西五台山，终于找到了佛光寺。他们看到了保存完好的佛光寺大殿：斗拱宏大（hóng），出檐深远，庄重质朴（pǔ），这都是唐代建筑的风格。他们还确定佛光寺的建造年代为公元857年。佛光寺是第一个被发现的唐代木结构建筑。

之后由于战争，梁思成生活困（kùn）苦，贫病交加。1944年，他在一个小山村里完成了《中国建筑史》，两年后又完成了英文版的《图像中国建筑史》。

资料

《图像中国建筑史》1946年完稿，1984年在美国出版。原名为 A Pictorial History of Chinese Architecture，获当年全美最优秀出版物的荣誉。

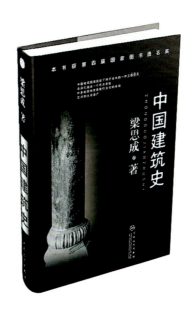

《营造法式》

《营造法式》由北宋李诫(jiè)编成,是中国第一本详细论述建筑工程做法的官方著作。书中规范(fàn)了各种建筑做法,详细规定了各种建筑施工(shī)设计、用料、结构、比例等方面的要求。全书357篇,3,555条,是当时建筑设计与施工经验的集合与总结,对后世产生深远影响。

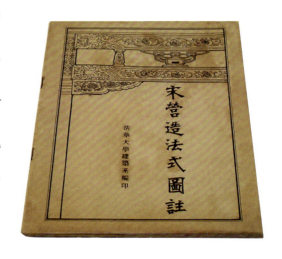

榫卯

榫卯中的"榫",是凸(tū)起物,"卯"是凹形,一凸一凹的扣合叫榫卯。中国古代在建筑和木结构制造工艺上不用钉子、胶水、绳子,而是用木头本身的榫卯进行勾连。

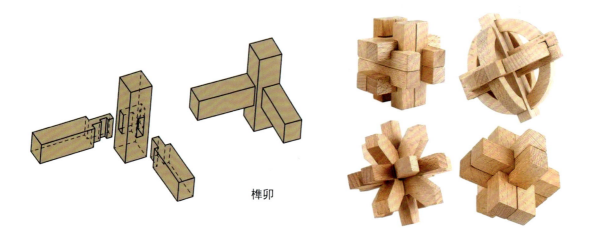

榫卯

Lesson Four

Ancient Chinese Architecture

China has a history of civilization for several thousand years. Its architecture of ancient palaces and temples has its distinct characteristics: the wooden frame structure and the large roof. The wooden frame structure is made by first compacting the soil to form a very solid foundation, then placing wooden posts and beams on top of it, and finally installing the roof.

The wooden frame structure of a building consists of columns, beams, and dougong (interlocking wooden brackets), the latter being a unique Chinese architectural feature and construction element. From both the artistic and the technical points of view, dougong can be called the essence of classical Chinese architecture. Dougong appeared in as early as the Zhou Dynasty. It is formed by a square block (dou) and a bow-shaped bracket (gong). By adding a gong onto dou and then adding another dou upon gong, layer by layer, the brackets form a support frame with the top bigger than the base which can bear heavy weight, supporting the "flying" eaves. The component pieces of the Chinese traditional wooden structure are joined together not by nails but by mortises and tenons, able to withstand strong earthquakes-as a saying goes, "The walls may fall but the house will not collapse." Take the Hall of Supreme Harmony inside the Imperial Palace for example, the roof of the hall, weighing two thousand tons, is supported by the wooden framed dougong. After withstanding several hundred years of winds and rains and earthquakes, it is still in perfect shape.

The giant roof of ancient Chinese architecture is most wondrous and greatly admired in the world. Think about it: the magnificent palace sits squarely upon the high foundation, secure and solemn; the soft curves of the giant roof, with the eaves tilting upward like a soaring bird, making the palace dignified elegant. The giant roof is not only beautiful, but also protects the doors, windows, and columns from rain and moisture.

At present, the biggest and most well-preserved ancient wooden architecture group in the whole world is the Imperial Palace in Beijing. The Imperial Palace, originally known as the Forbidden City, has a history of over 600 years. It covers an area of 720,000 square meters with more than 9,000 houses which form a sea of palaces. The roof of the palace is of golden glazed tiles that gleam in the sun. Under the golden eaves are colorful paintings of blue, green and white, red columns, doors and windows; the great hall sits on a foundation of white marbles, displaying a dazzling sight of gold and jade.

When we study the ancient Chinese architecture, we shouldn't forget Mr. Liang Sicheng. He was the pioneer for the study of the ancient Chinese architecture and spent his life in its preservation. He led a team that spent more than a decade systematically examining over one thousand ancient buildings in China and meticulously mapped the buildings in great detail. Later, he wrote *The History of Chinese*

Architecture and *A Pictorial History of Chinese Architecture* in English to introduce to China and the world the historical development and glorious achievements of the ancient Chinese architecture. Seeing his architectural drawings, people cannot help respecting him. Incorporating traditional Chinese brushwork techniques, his drawings wonderfully express the unique beauty of ancient Chinese architecture. His deep love for the ancient architecture manifested in every stroke of the drawing can move people to tears. He documented the ancient craftsmen and reclaimed the arts and skills of the ancient architecture that otherwise would have been lost.

Liang Sicheng and Buddha Light Temple

Liang Sicheng (1901-1972) was a famous Chinese architect, the pioneer in the study of the ancient Chinese architecture. In his early years of studying in the department of architecture in University of Pennsylvania in United States, he found that despite being a country of ancient civilization, China didn't have a single book on its architectural history written by Chinese themselves. So, he resolved to write a book on the history of Chinese Architecture. At that time, some Japanese scholars believed that the Tang Dynasty buildings with wooden structure had all been extinct in China.

Starting from 1931, Liang Sicheng led a small group, inspected more than 1,000 buildings in more than 200 cities and townships, and meticulously surveyed and mapped the majority of the buildings. Luckily in 1937, Sicheng Liang found the Buddha Light Temple in the *Drawing of Wutai Mountain* in the Tang Dynasty Cave Drawings in Dunhuang. He was very excited about the discovery and believed that China still had buildings of wooden structure of Tang Dynasty. Therefore, he and his wife Lin Huiyin and assistants started off to the Wutai Mountain in Shanxi, and finally they discovered the Buddha Light Temple. They saw the well-kept main hall of the Buddha Light Temple with its grand arch, far-reaching eaves, solemn and simple, all showing the style of Tang Dynasty architecture. They also dated the construction to 875 AD. The Buddha Light Temple is the first wooden structured architecture of Tang Dynasty to be found.

Afterwards, because of the war, Liang Sicheng suffered from poverty and disease. In 1944, in a small village, he finished *The History of Chinese Architecture*. Two years later, he finished the book in English of *A Pictorial History of Chinese Architecture*.

The Rules and Forms for Construction

The Rules and Forms for Construction was compiled by Li Jie in the Northern Song Dynasty. It was the first official book in China that expounds in detail the practice of building construction. The book standardizes various building methods and specifies in detail the requirements of various building construction designs, materials, structures, proportions, etc.. Containing 357 articles and 3,555 entries, it was a collection and summary of the architectural design and construction experiences at that time, and has profoundly influenced the later generations.

Mortise and Tenon

The "mortise" in mortise and tenon is a convex object, and the "tenon" is a concave shape. A convex and concave clasp are called the mortise and tenon.

The people did not use nails, glue, or string for the architecture and wooden structure in ancient times but the mortise and tenon to join wood pieces.

第五课

京 剧

京剧诞生在北京，有200多年的历史，是中国最流行的剧种。京剧，道白美，唱腔美，动作美，化妆美，服装美，处处是美。

京剧不像歌剧，只唱歌不跳舞；也不像舞蹈，只跳舞不唱歌。京剧艺术包括了"唱、念、做、打"四个方面的表演：

唱：是曲调演唱。

念：是剧中角色的对话和独白。

做：是表情和动作的表演。

打：是用舞蹈化的武术表演对打。

京剧的唱腔非常独特，表现力很强。京剧的道白声音时高时低，吐字时长时短，简直是音乐化的语言。京剧的虚拟表演动作更是一绝，一只桨可以代表一条船，一根马鞭可以代表骑马。演员不需要任何道具就能表演上楼、下楼、开门、关门等动作，这些动作虽然有些夸张，但是能给观众既优美又艺术的感觉。

京剧的演员分生、旦、净、丑四个行当。

"生"扮演男人，分老生、小生和武生。

"旦"扮演女人，又分青衣、花旦、武旦、老旦等。梅兰芳(lán)，就是著名的青衣演员。

"净"扮演性格豪放的男人，特点是要往脸上勾画花脸，所以也叫"花脸"。

"丑"扮演的是幽默机智或狡猾的男人。

生　　　　旦　　　　净　　　　丑

说到京剧，人们马上会想到"脸谱"，这是用夸张的画法来表现人物品德和性格的一种方法。"净"的脸谱勾画，一般忠勇

关公　　　　曹操　　　　蒋干

的人要画红脸，奸诈的人要画白脸。"丑"的脸谱，只把眼睛和鼻子画白，称为"小花脸"。

再看看京剧的服饰，可说是绚丽多彩。武生身穿丝袍(xuàn)，背后插着四面小旗。人物舞动，小旗子翻飞，流光闪闪，处处是神气。旦角的服饰更加艳丽：鲜艳的丝袍，绣着各种花卉，白色水袖甩动，光彩照人。

京剧有许多优秀剧目，如《贵妃醉酒》《三岔口(chà)》等。到中国旅游，不要忘了看京剧，去听一种完全不同于西方的曲调，看一套让人心动的虚拟表演，加上高超的武打、夸张的脸谱和唯美的京剧服饰，那是何等的过瘾！最美京剧——中国的国粹，艺术世界的一朵奇花！

京剧武生

京剧《白蛇传》

生词

chàng qiāng 唱腔	music for voices	yōu mò 幽默	humorous
huà zhuāng 化妆	makeup	liǎn pǔ 脸谱	facial makeup
qǔ diào 曲调	tune	zhōng yǒng 忠勇	loyal and brave
biǎo xiàn 表现	express	jiān zhà 奸诈	treacherous
xū nǐ 虚拟	virtual	fú shì 服饰	costume
jiǎng 桨	paddle	huā huì 花卉	flowers
yǎn yuán 演员	actor, actress	wéi měi 唯美	beautiful
chǒu 丑	ugly	guò yǐn 过瘾	satisfy a craving
xìng gé 性格	character	guó cuì 国粹	quintessence
háo fàng 豪放	bold		

听写

唱腔　化妆　曲调　演员　丑　性格　幽默

脸谱　服饰　花卉　国粹　*奸诈　唯美

比一比

勾（勾画）／沟（水沟）

虚｛虚拟／虚心｝

谱｛脸谱／乐谱｝

反义词

虚拟——真实　　　幽默——单调

夸张——真实　　　奸诈——老实

多音字

调 diào
曲调(diào)　调动(diào)

调 tiáo
调皮(tiáo)　调味料(tiáo)

词语运用

过瘾

① 这场足球赛踢得很激烈，看得真过瘾！

② 香港是美食天堂，我们吃得很过瘾。

③ 在北京，我去了长城、天坛、十三陵，玩得很过瘾。

既……又……

① 京剧的脸谱既夸张又艺术。

② 上海的小笼包既好吃又不贵。

③ 昆明的天气既温暖又湿润，很舒服。

程英睿　画

词语解释

道白——戏曲中的说白。

独白——文学作品或戏曲中人物的内心表白。

道具——演出戏剧、电影时所用的器物。

夸张——夸大。

行当——戏剧术语，角色分类。

阅读

京剧艺术大师梅兰芳

梅兰芳

梅兰芳（1894—1961）是著名的京剧艺术大师。他在京剧中是旦角演员。他唱得好，动作美，扮相端庄秀丽，在表演艺术上可说是完美。他不仅表演成功，还对京剧进行了创新。他设计了新的唱腔，把昆曲中载歌载舞的表演方法引入京剧，为京剧创造了各式各样的舞蹈，如绸舞、剑舞等。他在京剧的音乐伴奏上加入了二胡，丰富了京剧的音乐。除了这些，他还对人物的面部化妆、头饰和服装也都做了创新。这些使梅兰芳在舞台上容貌美、服装美、身段美、唱腔美，无一处不美。他使京剧表演显示了中国古典美的理想境界。梅兰芳还曾到过美国、欧洲和日本等地访问演出，受到了观众的喜爱和赞美。

《贵妃醉酒》，梅兰芳饰演

资料

中国地方戏

中国戏曲历史悠久。由于中国地域辽阔，各地的方言不同，除京剧外，还有许多种地方戏，比如：越剧（浙江）、黄梅戏（安徽）、粤剧（广东）等。地方戏都具有自己独特的风格，是当地人们喜爱的剧种。昆曲，是汉族传统戏曲中最古老的剧种之一，也是戏曲艺术中的珍品。

越剧《红楼梦》剧照

歌曲《唱脸谱》（片段）

外国人，把那京戏，叫作Beijing—Opera，

没见过那五色的油彩，愣往脸上画，

"四击头"一亮相，美极啦，妙极啦，简直OK，顶呱呱！

蓝脸的窦尔敦盗御马，红脸的关公战长沙，

黄脸的典韦，白脸的曹操，黑脸的张飞，叫——喳——喳！

中国民俗与民间艺术

Lesson Five

Peking Opera

Originating in Beijing, with a history of more than 200 years, Peking Opera is the most popular form of Chinese opera. It has beautiful speaking, beautiful singing, beautiful acting, beautiful make-ups, beautiful costumes—every element of the art form is utterly beautiful.

Unlike Western operas which have only singing but no dancing, or dances which has no singing, Peking Opera consists of four forms of performances: singing, speaking, acting, and combating.

Singing refers to singing in tunes.

Speaking is the conversations and monologues by the roles in the opera.

Acting means facial expressions and body language performance.

Combating is using choreographed martial arts to perform fights.

The aria of Peking Opera is very unique and highly expressive. The speaking voice is sometimes high and sometimes low, and the articulating is sometimes slow and sometimes abrupt, making the narrating very musical. The acting stimulated virtual imagery of Peking Opera is a unique feature —an oar can stand for a boat, and a whip, riding a horse. Actors do not need any props to perform movements such as going up or down the stairs, opening or closing doors, etc.. Although these movements are a bit exaggerated, they are graceful and artistic, giving the audience great pleasure.

Peking Opera features four main role types, sheng (male character), dan (female character), jing (painted-face), and chou (clown).

"Sheng" plays male characters of which there are three types: laosheng (old men), xiaosheng (young men), and wusheng (warriors).

"Dan" refers to women, divided into four subtypes of Qingyi (main female role), Huadan (vivacious and unmarried women), Wudan (female warriors), and Laodan (elderly women). Mei Lanfang was a very famous performer of Qingyi.

The Jing (painted face) performs the bold and uninhibited male roles, characterized with a painted face, therefore also called Hualian (painted face).

The Chou (clown) plays a humorous, witty or cunning male.

Speaking of Peking Opera, the first thing that comes to one's mind is its "facial makeup", a technique using exaggerated colors and distinctive patterns to show the characters' moral character. The facial makeup for the painted face generally follows the rule that the faces of the loyal and brave are drawn red; the faces of the treacherous, white. For the "clown" faces, they have a little white patch of paint on their eyes and noses, and they are also called Xiao Hualian (little painted face).

Now let's take a look at the Peking Opera costumes which are really gorgeous. Martial men are dressed in silk robes with four small flags on the back. The character dances and moves; flags flap

and fly; colors and lights flow and shine; the whole person embodies high spirit. The costumes for the female roles are even more striking. Embroidered with various flowers, with the white water-sleeves flailing, the bright silk robes shine splendidly.

The Peking Opera has many excellent plays such as *the Concubine Gets Drunk* and *The Three Forks*. When you visit China, don't forget to watch a Peking Opera in which you can listen to tunes completely different from the Western music and watch a mind-blowing virtual acting. What joy and fun it will be to see the superb martial arts, the exaggerated facial expressions, and the beautiful Peking Opera costumes! The beautiful Peking Opera is indeed a Chinese national treasure, a unique flower in the world of art!

Mei Lanfang, the Great Master of Peking Opera

Mei Lanfang(1894-1961) was a famous master of Peking Opera. He played the roles of Dan in Peking Opera. He sang wonderfully and danced beautifully; the characters played by him were dignified and beautiful. His performance was almost perfect. He was not only a successful performer, but also a reformer of Peking Opera. He created new ways of singing, introduced into Peking Opera the performing method unique to Kun Opera of dancing while singing, created all sorts of dances such as silk dance, sword dance for Peking Opera. He enriched the musical accompaniment of Peking Opera with the addition of the instrument Erhu. Besides these, he also made innovations to the characters' facial makeup, head decorations and costumes. All of these helped make the characters performed by him beautiful from head to toe: the face, costumes, body, and singing, all magnificent. His performing art manifested the ideal level of classic Chinese beauty. Mei Lanfang once visited and performed in America, Europe, and Japan where he was warmly appreciated and admired by the audience.

第六课

茶

中国有句俗话:"开门七件事——柴米油盐酱醋茶。"可见人们生活中不可一日无茶。朋友来了,端一杯清茶待客;饭后一杯茶帮助消化。喝茶健康又让人心平气和,茶真是中国人的好朋友。

中国是茶的故乡,种茶、制茶、饮茶都是最早的。《茶经》上说:"茶之为饮,发乎神农氏。"传说,一天神农在山中尝百草,口渴了,便在野茶树下烧水喝。一阵风吹来,几片树叶落入开水中,水变成了淡黄色。神农尝了尝,水带清香,喝下后,顿觉神清气爽,从此便有了茶。

神农

中国人喝茶有三千多年的历史了。最早,茶为药用,可以解毒。《神农本草经》中说:"神农尝百草,日遇七十二毒,得茶而解之。"公元7世纪,茶才成了家家户户的饮料。唐朝茶叶专家陆羽,小时候上山砍柴手常被划破,腿被虫子叮咬,红肿生疮,但是把茶叶捣烂敷(fū)上,不久就好了。有时他吃了野果,

第六课

《唐人宫乐图》摹本

上吐下泻，也是喝了茶汤才治好的。陆羽觉得茶很神奇，不仅好喝，还能入药。他花了多年时间写了一本介绍茶叶的书——《茶经》，让天下人都了解茶，喜欢茶，帮助人们强健身体。后来，人们称他为"茶神陆羽"。

同是茶树叶子，中国茶因制作工艺不同可分为：绿茶、红茶、乌龙茶、黑茶、黄茶和白茶六大类。这里我们介绍其中的四类。

绿茶，是不发酵茶，茶汤淡黄绿色，味道清香。著名的绿茶有西湖龙井等。

红茶，是全发酵茶，汤色红艳明亮。著名的红茶有祁(qí)门红茶等。红茶也是世界上销售最多的茶。

乌龙茶，是半发酵茶，茶汤橙黄明亮，有着千变万化的香。著名的乌龙茶有"大红袍""铁观音"等。

黑茶，是发酵时间最长的茶，汤色红浓明亮，是游牧民族的生命之饮。知名的黑茶有普洱(ěr)茶。

除了六大类茶，中国人还爱喝花茶。花茶，是把花和茶放在一起制作而成的，茉莉花茶很有名。

谈到喝茶，水非常重要。古人说："茶要新，水要活。"活水，就是流水。陆羽说："山泉为上，江水次之，井水为下。"在中国杭州就有这样的说法："虎跑（páo）泉水泡龙井茶是最好的。"

采茶姑娘

喝茶，还讲究茶具。茶具有瓷器的，有陶制的和玻璃的……其中陶具常常成为饮茶人的至爱，比如宜兴的紫砂泥壶。

在中国云南、四川、安徽、浙江、福建等省都有大片的茶园。不论南方或北方，长期以来人们都有饮茶的习惯，可以说茶是中国人最喜欢的饮料。

陶制茶具（谢光辉摄）

生词

chái 柴	firewood		hóng zhǒng 红肿	red and swollen
cù 醋	vinegar		shēng chuāng 生疮	sore
bēi 杯	cup		shàng tù xià xiè 上吐下泻	vomiting and diarrhea
shuǎng 爽	refresh		fā jiào 发酵	ferment
yǐn liào 饮料	drinks		hóng yàn 红艳	red and bright
zhuān jiā 专家	expert		xiāo shòu 销售	sell
huá pò 划破	scratch		chéng 橙	orange
dīng yǎo 叮咬	bite		jiǎng jiu 讲究	pay attention to

听写

醋　杯　爽　饮料　专家　划破　叮咬　红肿

上吐下泻　发酵　销售　橙　*红艳　讲究

比一比

饮 { 饮茶 / 饮酒 / 饮料 }　　专 { 专家 / 专门 / 专业 }　　售 { 销售 / 售卖 / 出售 }

| 杯子 | 怀里 | 坏了 |

反义词

讲究——随便　　　　明亮——暗淡

组词组字游戏

酱

酱油——果子酱——苹果酱——花生酱——桃子酱
甜面酱——芝麻酱——酱牛肉——酱鸭——炸酱面

此木为柴　　山石为岩
女子为好　　古木为枯

第六课

词语运用

销售

① 红茶在世界上是销售最多的茶。

② 今年汽车的销售比去年好。

③ 哥哥在公司里是负责服装销售的经理。

讲究

① 泡茶还讲究水,山泉最好,自来水没法比。

② 写汉字讲究横平竖直。

③ 中国人讲究吃,会花很多时间做饭。

词语解释

故乡——出生或长期生活的地方。

茶具——指茶壶、茶杯、茶碗、茶盘等饮茶用具。

至爱——最爱的。

茶文化*

茶在中国有三千多年历史了。7世纪时，茶成为家家户户不可缺(quē)少的饮品。后来城市里出现了茶馆。朋友们在茶馆里一边喝茶聊天，一边看节目听故事。茶馆是休闲(xián)和朋友聚会的好地方。在百姓家庭中，客人来访，端上一杯茶，是中国人的礼仪和习俗。

茶是一种健康的饮品。茶性温和，可以提神、助消化，利于健康。人们也常举行茶会，以茶代酒交友。

茶文化还表现在中国人的哲(zhé)学思想中。有人说中国人的性格像茶：清醒平和，社会生活中主张和谐(xié)理性。

公园中的茶馆

---

*茶文化包括茶道、茶德、茶书、茶具、茶故事、茶艺等。

龙井茶　虎跑泉

龙井茶产自浙江。"龙井"是茶名，是地名，是村名，也是泉名。那里的古人认为，"龙井"这口井与海相通，其中有龙，所以叫龙井。龙井茶是不发酵的绿茶。绿茶是中国人喜欢的茶。

龙井茶

离杭州不远，有一个虎跑泉。传说是两个仙童化作两只老虎，刨(páo)出了一股清泉，起名虎跑泉。古往今来，人们到杭州旅游时，大都会品尝一下虎跑泉水冲泡的龙井茶。

虎跑泉

中国民俗与民间艺术

资料

六大茶类

白茶、绿茶、黄茶、红茶、乌龙茶、黑茶：
白茶，不发酵茶，不炒(chǎo)不揉(róu)，保留了天然的原味；
绿茶，不发酵茶，保持了茶的鲜度；
黄茶，轻微发酵的茶，比绿茶多了一分柔和；
乌龙茶，半发酵茶，有着千变万化的香；
红茶，全发酵茶，是世界上销售最多的茶；
黑茶，发酵时间最长的茶，是游牧民族的生命之饮。

草原牧民与茶

中国的内蒙古草原和青藏高原都不产茶，可是那里的牧民却有天天喝茶的习惯。这是为什么呢？原来牧民们饮食单一，每天除了肉就是奶，吃不到水果和蔬(shū)菜，所以常常便秘，肚子痛。而茶能够帮助消化，茶里的维生素和微量元素正好是牧民食物中缺少的。所以牧民不能缺少茶。草原上有句话："宁可三日无粮，不可一日无茶；一日无茶则滞(zhì)，三日无茶则病。"茶是饮品也是"药"，是牧民的生命线。

牧民敬茶

《茶经》

《茶经》是世界上最早、最完整、最全面介绍茶的专著，被称为茶叶百科全书，唐代陆羽所著。

此书是关于茶叶生产的历史、源流、现状、生产技术以及饮茶技艺、茶道原理的综合性茶学专著，也是阐述茶文化的书，将普通茶事升格为美妙的文化艺术，推动了中国茶文化的发展。

茶神陆羽　　　　　　　　　　　　　　　王金泰　画

饮茶活动

准备工作

1. 茶叶：绿茶、红茶、乌龙茶、花茶等（4种至6种）；
2. 茶具：瓷茶具、陶制茶具等（1套至2套）；
3. 点心：品茶配的小点心（味道不要太重）；
4. 开水壶。

品茶步骤

1. 观看茶叶、茶汤、茶具；
2. 每人一杯茶，先闻香，听老师讲茶，小口品茶，之后吃点心，类推再品其他几种茶；
3. 茶品完后，做游戏：蒙上一位同学的眼睛，给他不同种类的茶来品，让他说出是哪种茶。

Lesson Six

Tea

A Chinese saying goes as "There are 7 essential matters when you open your door: firewood, rice, oil, salt, sauce, vinegar, and tea" which shows that tea is indispensable in daily life. When friends come for a visit, they are offered a cup of clear tea; after a meal, people drink a cup of tea to help digest the food. Drinking tea helps people stay healthy and calm. Tea is really a good friend for Chinese.

China is home to tea. The cultivating, processing, and drinking of tea all first appeared in China. *The Book of Tea* says: "Tea as a drink was started by Shennongshi." As the legend goes, one day, while Shennong was sampling plants in a mountain, he felt thirsty. So, he began to boil water under a wild tea tree. With a gust of wind, several leaves fell into the boiling water, and the color of the water changed into pale yellow. Shennong tasted the water and found it aromatic. After drinking it, he felt calm and refreshed. From then on, tea came into being.

The history of tea drinking in China has been over three thousand years. In the very beginning, tea was used as a medicine to detoxify poisons. As *Shennong Classic of Materia Medica* says, when Shennong tasted plants, he was poisoned 72 times in a day but each time the poison was detoxified by tea. In the 7th century, tea became a household drink. In Tang Dynasty there was a tea expert called Lu Yu who, as a young boy, went to the mountain every day to chop woods. His hands were often scratched and his legs got swelling sores from insect bites. Each time, after he put on mashed tea leaves the wounds would soon heal. Sometimes he vomited and had diarrhea after he ate wild fruits and berries, but after drinking some tea, he would recover. Lu Yu felt that tea was miraculous as it not only tasted good but also could cure diseases. He spent many years writing a book about tea called *the Book of Tea*, which helped people all over the country to know about tea, to enjoy drinking tea, and to become strong and healthy. Later people began to call him Lu Yu the God of Tea.

After the leaves are hand-picked from tea trees, they are processed in different procedures and become six types of tea, i.e., green tea, black tea, oolong tea, dark tea, yellow tea, and white tea. Here we introduce four kinds of them.

Green tea is inoxidized. The tea broth looks pale yellow greenish and has a fresh aroma. Xihu Longjing (West Lake Longjing tea) is a famous green tea.

Black tea is fully oxidized. The tea broth looks red and bright. Qimen Black Tea is a very famous black tea brand. Black tea is also the bestselling tea worldwide.

Oolong tea is half oxidized. Its broth looks orange and bright, has an aroma of many variations. Famous oolong tea brands are "Dahongpao" "Tieguanyin" and so on.

Dark tea is oxidized for the longest time. Its broth is red, thick, and bright. It's the drink of life for nomads. Pu'er is a famous dark tea.

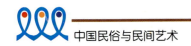

Besides the six types of tea, Chinese also love to drink the scented tea. Scented tea is made together with tea and flower. Jasmine tea is very famous.

Speaking of drinking tea, water is very important. Ancient people said that "Tea needs to be fresh; water needs to be alive." "Alive water" is the running water. Lu Yu said the best water is from mountain springs; the mediocre water, rivers; the worst water, wells. In Hangzhou of China, people say that water from Hupao Spring is the best for making Longjing tea.

The tea set is also essential to drinking tea. There are tea sets made of porcelain, ceramic, as well as glass, among which the ceramic tea set such as the purple soil tea pot from Yixing is often the favorite for tea drinkers.

There are large tea plantations in the provinces of Yunan, Sichuan, Anhui, Zhejiang, and Fujian in China. No matter in the South or North, people have the long-lasting habit of drinking tea. We can say that tea is the favorite drink for Chinese.

The Tea Culture

Tea has a history of more than 3,000 years in China. In the 7th century, tea became the indispensable drink for every household. Later in cities tea houses came into being. Friends talk and drink tea in the tea house while watching performances and listening to stories. The tea house is a good place to go in leisure times and to meet with friends. In ordinary families, when friends come to visit, offering them a cup of tea is the Chinese etiquette and tradition.

Tea is a healthy drink. It is mild, refreshing, helpful for digestion, and good for health. People often hold tea parties, making friends while drinking tea instead of wine.

The tea culture is also expressed in Chinese philosophy. Some say the national character of Chinese is like tea: sober and calm, advocating harmony and reason in social life.

Longjing Tea and Hupao Spring

Longjing tea is from Zhejiang Province. Longjing is the name for the tea, for the place, for the village, and for the spring. People living there in the old times believed that this well was connected with the sea and inside the well there was a dragon, hence the name of Longjing—dragon well. Longjing tea is an unfermented green tea favored by Chinese people.

Not far from Hangzhou, there is a Hupao Spring. The legend goes that two fairy boys transformed into two tigers and dug out a clear spring named the Hupao Spring. From the ancient times to the present, most visitors to Hangzhou will enjoy the Longjing tea made with water from the Hupao Spring.

Grassland Herders and Tea

There is no tea in Inner Mongolia Grassland and Tibetan Plateau, but the herders there have the habit of drinking tea every day. Why is it? The reason is the herders have a single diet of meat and milk with no fruits and vegetable. As a result, they often suffer from constipation and stomachache. Tea

can help digestion as its vitamins and trace elements are exactly what the herders lack in their food. Therefore, the herders cannot go without tea. There is a saying in the grasslands that "One can live for three days without food, but not a single day without tea. Not drinking tea for one day will lead to constipation; for three days will lead to disease." Tea is not only a drink but also a medicine, a lifeline for the herders.

The Book of Tea

The Book of Tea is the earliest, most comprehensive book specifically on tea in the entire world. Written by Lu Yu in Tang Dynasty, it is called the encyclopedia of tea.

A treatise on tea, the book expounds the tea culture, covers its history, origin, contemporary conditions, production technology, drinking techniques and the principles of tea ceremony. It has elevated the simple tea drinking to exquisite cultural art and promoted the development of tea culture in China.

第七课

中国菜

中国菜在世界上是深受各国人民喜爱的。中国菜不但花样多，还讲究色、香、味俱全。

由于中国地域辽阔，各地气候不同，物产和生活习惯不同，人们的口味也不相同。比如：北方人爱吃面，南方人爱吃米；北方人吃咸，南方人吃甜；四川人吃辣，广东人吃鲜……这就形成了各地的风味菜：山东菜"葱烧海参（shēn）"，广东菜"清蒸鱼"，四川菜"麻婆豆腐"等等。还有各地风味小吃：上海小笼包、新疆羊肉串、北京春饼等，说也说不完。下面我们就说说深受中国人喜爱的大众食品和进餐习惯。

好吃不过饺子

饺子，是中国百姓千家万户的传统美食，已有一千多年历史了。平时人们的家庭聚会，招待客人，常常吃饺子。都说"好吃不过饺子"，别看酒席上一道道大

菜,最后饺子一来,还是挺受欢迎的。在中国,饺子也是年节食品,冬至和春节都有吃饺子的习惯。

饺子好吃,做起来也不算麻烦:是用面皮儿包馅儿,水煮而成,所以也叫水饺。饺子馅儿有各种各样的:菜肉馅儿、鱼肉馅儿、三鲜馅儿、素馅儿等等。俗话说:"有钱没钱,吃饺子过年。"意思是过年每个人一定得吃饺子。除夕那天,全家一起包饺子,聊天,看节目,直到新的一年开始。吃饺子,过年啦!

北京烤鸭

到北京旅游有这样的说法:"不到长城非好汉,不吃烤鸭真遗憾!"当你坐在老字号"全聚德"烤鸭店时,看到的是用果木烤出的鸭子。烤鸭金黄油亮,外酥里嫩,还带有果木香气。最新奇的是厨师当众片鸭,鸭肉被片成小薄片,有皮有肉,十分讲究。吃烤鸭是有方法的:取一张小薄饼,抹上一点儿甜面酱,放几根葱丝,几片鸭肉,再把饼卷好入口,真过瘾。鸭子吃完,还可以尝一尝鲜美的鸭架汤。吃完烤鸭的客人,个个面带微笑,挺

北京烤鸭

着肚子满意地离开，心里盘算着下次再来。

菜名的故事

中国菜名五花八门，许多菜名是有故事的。比如天津著名的"狗不理"包子，原是一种皮薄馅儿嫩、又香又软、十分可口的肉包子。为什么这么好吃的包子叫"狗不理"？

天津狗不理

"狗不理"餐馆诞生于160多年前，原店名叫德聚号，老板是一位小名叫"狗子"的年轻人。他包子做得好，顾客越来越多，因为忙着做包子，也顾不上和顾客说话。于是顾客都戏称他为"狗子卖包子，不理人"。"狗不理"因此得名。这个名称一直叫到今天，成了天津的老字号。

进餐习惯

在中国人看来，吃饭不仅是吃饱，吃好，还是家庭团聚和交友的一部分。中国人是家人围坐一起吃饭，相互夹菜，边吃边聊，很温馨。如有客人，主人会给客人夹菜，表达尊重和关怀。节日里，家人围在一起吃团圆饭，长辈给晚辈夹菜，晚辈给长辈敬酒，热热闹闹。吃饭重要的是吃出气氛，吃出感情。

第七课

生词

俱全 jù quán	complete	遗憾 yí hàn	regret
辣 là	spicy	酥 sū	crispy
葱 cōng	scallion	嫩 nèn	tender
蒸 zhēng	steam	抹 mǒ	wipe
豆腐 dòu fu	bean curd	顾客 gù kè	customer
聚会 jù huì	party	饱 bǎo	full
招待 zhāo dài	entertain	温馨 wēn xīn	sweet
挺 tǐng	very, quite; stick out	尊重 zūn zhòng	respect
馅儿 xiànr	filling		

听写

俱全　辣　葱　豆腐　聚会　招待　挺　馅儿

遗憾　抹　顾客　饱　尊重　*蒸　温馨

比一比

餐 { 餐厅 / 餐馆 }　　聚 { 聚会 / 团聚 }　　顾 { 顾客 / 顾不上 }

| 餐 | 聚 | 馨 |

餐厅　　　聚会　　　温馨

反义词

麻烦——简单　　　饱——饿
遗憾——圆满　　　聚——散

词语运用

遗憾

① 明天北京有雨，真遗憾不能去长城了。

② 去西安玩儿，看过兵马俑就没什么遗憾了。

③ 到北京旅游，没吃烤鸭真遗憾！

顾不上

① 妈妈从早忙到晚，常常连饭都顾不上吃。

② 老板忙着做包子，顾不上和客人说话。

③ 要迟到了，他什么也顾不上，开车就走。

组词游戏

挺

挺好——挺坏——挺深——挺浅——挺冷的——挺热的

挺麻烦——挺讨厌——挺可爱——挺漂亮——挺像的

挺香的——挺饱的——挺饿的——挺舒服——挺难受

挺遗憾——挺满足——挺能干——挺开朗——挺闭塞

词语解释

老字号——指有很长历史的店铺。

五花八门——原指打仗阵式，现比喻花样多。

敬酒——祝酒。

阅读

东坡肉

浙江有一道名菜叫东坡肉。是北宋大诗人苏东坡在杭州做官时创制的。在清理西湖时，苏东坡做了红烧肉犒(kào)劳干活儿的百姓，后来人们就把这种红烧肉叫东坡肉。

中国菜式顺口溜

北京烤鸭，小笼包，
麻婆豆腐，炒年糕。
清蒸鱼，核桃虾，
宫保鸡丁，铁板烧。

资料

饺子的做法（菜肉馅儿）

用料：面粉500克、碎肉300克、鸡蛋2个、白菜叶7片、葱3根、姜(jiāng)1小块；盐、料酒、酱油备用。

1 和(huó)面：用温水将面揉成面团，再醒30分钟。

2 调馅儿：碎肉加鸡蛋，少许水调开，加入盐、酱油、料酒、姜末、葱碎，调匀。白菜切碎，挤(jǐ)水后和肉馅儿混合。

3 擀(gǎn)皮儿：醒好的面团，做成多个圆形小面皮儿。

4 包饺子：用面皮儿包上肉馅儿，捏成月牙形。

5 煮饺子：一锅水煮开，饺子下入锅内，轻轻搅动，使饺子不粘锅底。水再开时，倒入一些凉水，反复三次，水饺(jiǎo)已熟，捞出上盘食用。

Lesson Seven

Chinese Cuisine

Chinese cuisine is well liked by people in many countries. It has not only many varieties, but also stresses the combination of presentation, aroma, and taste.

China is a vast country with different climates, produces, and customs. People in different regions have different tastes. For example, people in the North like food made from wheat flour, whereas people in the South prefer rice; northerners like salty food, southerners, sweet; people in Sichuan like hot and spicy food, people in Guangdong, fresh taste. Different regions have different famous dishes. For example, Shandong Province has a famous dish called Braised Sea Cucumber with Shallots; Guangdong Province has one called Plain Steamed Fish; Sichuan one called Mapo Tofu (stir-fried bean curd in chili sauce). There are also many special flavored snacks such as Shanghai steamed dumplings, Xinjiang lamb skewers, Beijing spring pancakes and so on. It's impossible to name them all.

Now we first talk about the popular foods loved by all Chinese people and the eating habits.

Nothing Is More Delicious than Dumplings

For more than one thousand years, dumplings are the traditional gourmet for all Chinese households. People often eat dumplings in usual family gatherings and when treating guests. People say, "Nothing is more delicious than dumplings!" Although there are many entrees in a banquet, people still like dumplings the most when they are finally served. In China, dumplings are also special food for festivals. On Winter Solstice and the Spring Festival, people have the tradition of eating dumplings.

Dumplings are very delicious and not too troublesome to make: put fillings inside wraps of thin dough paste, boil them in water, voila, ready to serve. So, it is also called "water dumplings". The dumpling fillings have a lot of varieties: mixture of vegetable and meat, minced fish fillings, three ingredients fillings, vegetable fillings, etc. As an old saying goes, "Rich or poor, all eat dumplings to celebrate the Chinese New Year." It means for the Chinese New Year everyone shall eat dumplings. On the Eve of the Chinese Yew Year, the whole family sit together to make dumplings, talk with each other, watch TV shows until the New Year begins. Then they will eat dumplings. The New Year has come!

Beijing Roast Duck

There is a saying for visitors to Beijing that "You are not a strong man if you don't climb the Great Wall; it's a real pity if you don't eat Beijing roast duck." When you sit in the original Quanjude roast duck restaurant, you will see ducks roasted with fruit tree branches. The roasted duck is golden, shining with oil, crispy on the outside yet tender and juicy on the inside, smelling of the aroma of fruit tree. The most eye-catching scene is the cook slicing the roasted duck before diners. The duck is sliced into thin pieces with skin and meat all in a plate and eaten in a particular way. This is the way to eat the roasted duck: take a thin steamed pancake, spread on it some sweet bean sauce, put on a few shreds of green onion, several pieces of duck meat, roll them up, and then put the wrapped roll into the mouth. What a delicious treat! After eating the duck, you can also drink the delicious soup made from the duck bones. After eating the roast duck, every customer leaves with a smile on the face and a satisfied belly, planning to come back next time.

Stories about Dish Names

Chinese dishes have lots of interesting names. Many names have stories about them. For example, the famous Tianjin "Goubuli (the dog doesn't bother)" buns with fillings are basically very delicious buns with thin flour skin stuffed with soft and tender meat fillings. Why are such delicious buns with fillings called "Goubuli (the dog doesn't bother)"? The restaurant of "Goubuli" was founded over 160 years ago. The original restaurant was called "Dejuhao (virtue gathering)", the owner of which was a young man nicknamed "Gouzi(doggie)". He was very good at making buns with fillings, so he had more and more customers. Because he was so busy making buns, he didn't have time to chat with customers. So, his customers jokingly said about him that "Gouzi (Doggie) sells buns, not bothering to talk with people". Hence the name of "Goubuli (the dog doesn't bother)" came into being. The name has survived since then and becomes a time-honored trade mark in Tianjin.

Eating Habits

For Chinese, eating a meal doesn't only mean to stuff the stomach with nice dishes. It is also a part of gathering with family members and making friends. When Chinese eat a meal, all family members sit around a table and help each other to dishes, talking while eating, enjoying a very warm and relaxing atmosphere. When guests are present, the host shall help the guests to the dishes to show them respect and care. On holidays, family members sit around a table to eat a meal of reunion during which the elders pick up food for the children and the children propose toasts to the elders. The meal is bustling with energy and warmth. What's important about eating a meal is to create a warm atmosphere and mutual affection.

Dongpo Pork

In Zhejiang Province, there is a famous dish called Dongpo Pork. It was created and first made by the great poet Su Dongpo in Northern Song Dynasty when he was an official in Hangzhou. When workers cleaned up the West Lake, Su Dongpo made this dish to treat everyone. Since then, people called this dish Dongpo Pork.

第八课

书法艺术

北京紫禁城有六百多年了，在太和殿的中央，有一把高高的龙椅。在龙椅的上方和两旁的柱子上，挂着匾额和楹(yíng)联。今天，皇帝早已无影无踪，可匾额楹联上精美的书法作品，却吸引着游客的目光。

书法是什么？简单地说就是用毛笔书写汉字的艺术。那么一种写字的方法为什么被称为艺术？

在中国，上过学的人都会写汉字，但用毛笔把汉字写好可不容易。一幅漂亮的字，像一幅画儿，看起来很美。汉字有各种结构，书写讲究匀称(zhèn)，笔画从一笔到几十笔。毛笔蘸上墨汁，在宣纸上书写，一笔下去，粗细、长短、浓淡、虚实，变化无穷。有些汉字，像小小的抽象画，配上字的意思，就有了意境。

北京故宫

比如"雨"字,诗人余光中写道:

"凭空写一个'雨'字,

点点滴滴,

滂滂沱沱(tuó),

淅淅沥沥(lì),

一切云情雨意就宛然其中了。"

因为有意境,汉字从诞生之日起,就有了自己的审美要求,在实用之外,走上了艺术美的方向,成为表达民族美感的一种方式。

在整篇书法作品中,字与字之间,行与行之间,也要讲究整体布局。常见的书法字体有:篆(zhuàn)书、隶书、楷书、草书和行书。现在我们最常用的是一笔一画写得很端正的楷书,还有介于楷书和草书之间的行书。

篆书　隶书　楷书　草书　行书

从古至今，中国出过许多著名的书法家，如王羲之(xī)、颜真卿(qīng)等。他们的作品虽然风格不同，但都非常动人。

汉瓦当拓片

书法作品除了是艺术品之外，也服务于中国人日常生活的方方面面。早在秦汉时期的瓦当文，已是书法作品了，一块块美丽的瓦当装饰着建筑物。还有宫殿、楼阁的牌匾，商铺的名牌，名山中的书法石刻，都是书法艺术。再看钱币，无论是春秋战国时期流行的布币、刀币，还是现在的人民币，钱币上使用的文字都是极其讲究书法艺术性的。

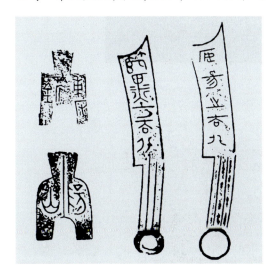
春秋战国布币、刀币

战国布币

清咸丰元宝

人民币

自古以来，人们写字作画离不开纸、墨、笔、砚。这四种文具被称为文房四宝。最著名的是宣纸、徽墨、湖笔和端砚。

文房四宝

生词

biǎn é 匾额	horizontal inscribed board	píng kōng 凭空	out of thin air
wú yǐng wú zōng 无影无踪	without a trace	wǎn rán 宛然	seem
yún chèn 匀称	symmetry	shěn měi 审美	aesthetic
mò zhī 墨汁	ink	bù jú 布局	layout
xuān zhǐ 宣纸	rice paper	lì shū 隶书	clerical script
xū shí 虚实	deficiency and excess	kǎi shū 楷书	regular script
chōu xiàng 抽象	abstract	míng pái 名牌	name plates; famous brand
yì jìng 意境	artistic conception	yàn tai 砚台	inkstone

听写

匾额　无影无踪　匀称　虚实　抽象　凭空　审美

布局　隶书　楷书　名牌　*墨汁　意境

比一比

额 { 匾额 / 额头 }　　宣 { 宣纸 / 宣传 }　　诞 { 诞生 / 圣诞节 }

扁	遍	篇	骗	匾
压扁	一遍	一篇	骗人	匾额

反义词

中央——四周　　　　抽象——具体

近义词

匾额——牌匾——门匾

故宫博物院

词语运用

除了……之外

① 除了你之外,别人都没迟到。

② 书包里除了书和本子之外还有一个饭盒。

③ 我除了参加游泳队之外,还参加了合唱团。

名牌

① 北京有些商铺的名牌是乾隆皇帝题写的。

② 北京画店的名牌是吴作人题写的。

词语解释

匾——题字的横牌,多挂在门或墙的上部。

楹联——题写在楹柱上的对联,也指对联。

吸引——把别人的注意力引到自己这方面来。

端正——不歪斜,各部分保持平衡。

中国民俗与民间艺术

阅读

王羲之和《兰亭集序》

东晋永和九年（公元353年）三月初三，大书法家王羲之邀谢安等四十一位朋友聚于会稽山阴的兰亭。大家坐在溪边，曲水流觞，饮酒作诗。书童将盛着酒的觞放入溪水中，顺水流动，酒觞停在谁面前，谁就要写诗一首，若写不出来，罚酒三杯。当日共写诗三十七首，汇编成集，这便是《兰亭集》。此时大家推王羲之为《兰亭集》作序。王羲之酒意正浓，提笔写下序文，共二十八行，三百二十四字，一气呵成。这就是著名的《兰亭集序》。序中记述了兰亭周围山水之美和聚会的欢乐之情。第二天，王羲之醒来，将序文再写一遍，却不如原文精妙。这篇序文已经是他一生中的顶峰之作。

曲水流觞

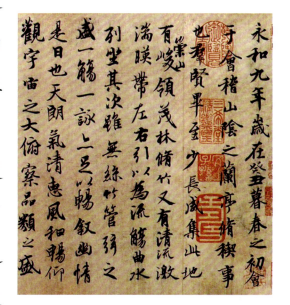

王羲之《兰亭集序》

资料

文房四宝

宣纸

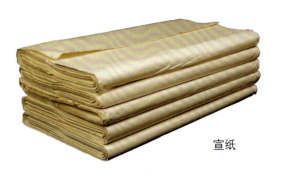
宣纸

宣纸是一种名贵的纸张，产在安徽宣城附近，所以叫宣纸。早在汉唐时代，宣纸已是给皇帝的贡(gòng)品了。宣纸洁白柔软，拉力大，吸水性强，最能表现出中国书法和水墨画的特点。由于宣纸可存放很长时间不破碎，不变色，所以我们今天还能看到几百年，甚至上千年前的古代字画。

徽墨

中国的书画家对用墨十分讲究。安徽徽州生产的墨最有名。徽墨从唐代开始生产已有1000多年历史了。在制作徽墨时加入香料，墨不但颜色黑润(rùn)，而且还有香气。

湖笔

文房四宝中的笔，指毛笔。毛笔的生产和使用已有几千年历史。一支好的毛笔，要经过70多道工序，笔上的毛要一根根地挑选。中国最有名的毛笔是浙江湖州生产的湖笔。

端砚

砚是研墨的工具,在中国已有3000多年历史。端砚是最有名的,产于广东省。用端溪的端石制成。

Lesson Eight

The Art of Calligraphy

The Forbidden City in Beijing has a history of six hundred years, inside which, in the middle of the hall of Supreme Harmony, there is a high throne. Above the throne and on the pillars on two sides, hang a horizontal inscribed board and couplets on scroll. Today, there is no trace of the emperors, but the beautiful artworks of calligraphy in the board and couplets still attract the eyes of visitors.

What is calligraphy? Simply put, it is the art of writing Chinese characters with a brush. Then why is a way of writing called an art?

In China, whoever has been to school can write Chinese characters. But it is not easy to write the characters nicely with a brush. A nice calligraphy is like a painting and looks very beautiful to the eye. Chinese characters have all kinds of structure, so in writing symmetry has to be paid particular attention to. The number of strokes in the characters ranges from one to several tens. People first dip the brush into the ink and then write on the rice paper. Within one stroke there are endless of variations in thickness, length, shades of color, and fullness. Some characters are like mini abstract paintings, embodying a lot of artistic beauty associated with their meanings.

Take the character of "yu(rain)" for an example. The poet Yu Guangzhong wrote, "Write a character of Rain on the empty paper. The little drops, the heavy shower, the fitful pattering, all the feelings of clouds and associations of rains are inside it."

Because of the innate artistic conception, since the day Chinese characters came into being, there have been aesthetic requirements for them. Besides having a pragmatic function, Chinese characters have evolved along the line of artistic beauty, becoming a way to express the sense of beauty for the whole nation.

Inside an entire piece of calligraphy artwork, alongside each character, between each line, the overall layout has to be carefully considered. The common calligraphy fonts are seal script, clerical script, regular script, cursive script, and running script. Nowadays, we most commonly use the regular script, every stroke of which is written very properly, and the running script, which is somewhere between the regular and cursive script.

From ancient times to the present, China has seen many famous calligraphers, such as Wang Xizhi, Yan Zhenqing and so on. Although their styles are different, all of their works are very appealing.

Besides being the works of art, calligraphy works also serve the Chinese people in many aspects of their daily lives. As early as in the Qin and Han Dynasty, the beautiful characters in the Eaves Tiles adorned the ancient architecture. There are calligraphic art works such as plaques in palaces and pavilions, name plates in shops, and calligraphic stone carvings in famous mountains. If we look at the coins, whether it is the cloth coins and knife coins populated in the Spring and Autumn Period and the Warring States Period or the current RMB, the characters on the money are all extremely artistic calligraphy works.

Since ancient times, paper, ink, brush and inkstone are indispensable when people write or draw. These four kinds of stationery are known as the Four Treasures of the Study. The most famous ones are rice paper made in Xuancheng (Anhui Province), inkstick from Huizhou (Anhui Province), ink brush from Huzhou (Zhejiang Province), and inkstone made in Duanxi (Guangdong Province).

Wang Xizhi and *LangTingji Xu* (*Preface to the Poems Composed at the Orchid Pavilion*)

On the 3rd day of March in lunar calendar, in the 9th year of Yonghe (353AD) in East Jin Dynasty, the great calligrapher Wang Xizhi invited 41 friends including Xie An to gather at the Orchid Pavilion in Shanyin county, Kuaiji prefecture. They sat along a winding brook, put the wine goblet in the flowing water, wrote poems and drank wine from the goblet. A book keeper put the goblet filled with wine into the brook; the goblet floated in the water. When it stopped in front of someone, he should come up with one poem. If he could not write the poem, he should drink three cups of wine as penalty. On that day 37 poems were written and put into one collection called *The Poems Composed at the Orchid Pavilion*. Wang Xizhi was selected by all to write the preface to the collection. Under the full influence of wine, he took a brush and wrote in one go the entire preface composed of 28 columns and 324 characters. This is the famous *LangTingji Xu* (*Preface to the Poems Composed at the Orchid Pavilion*), in which he described the beauty of the mountain and the water surrounding the Orchid Pavilion, and the joy of friends gathering together. On the following day, after waking up from the wine, Wang Xizhi rewrote the preface, but the writing was not as marvelous as the original which had become the pinnacle work of his life.

第九课

中国武术

武术是中国传统文化中的一颗明珠，也被称为国粹。武术历史悠久，源于民间，盛行于民间，著名的有少林拳、太极拳等。武术不仅是强身的运动，还包含厚重的人文思想，讲究教人行善、修身养性、追求和平等丰富的内容。

学习武术，老师先要教学生传统武德，明白习武的目的是：强身、自卫、除恶助弱，消停战事，求得和平。

现在，武术已成为深受人们喜爱的体育运动，许多项目也适合儿童、老年和体弱多病的人。比如：中学、大学里有武术队；全国中小学的课间有武术操；在体育学校里，设有武术教学和研究部门。体育馆中常举行各种武术比赛，电影和戏剧中的武术表演也很丰富，可以说武术对中国人生活的影响无处不在。学习武

李小龙

术讲究：站如松，坐如钟，行如风，一股精气神在身。大多数武术动作快而多变化，出拳、踢腿、飞跳，一招一式都透着中国武术特有的力量与东方美感。

太极拳是武术中的一种，在中国无人不知。练习太极拳讲究中定、放松、心静、慢练。清晨，在公园里，许多老年人和体弱的人打太极拳，动作和缓，如行云流水。当你认真打完一套太极拳，其实并不轻松，身上会发热并出些微汗。

武术对中国文学艺术的影响也很深远。首先是古典小说的许多英雄人物都武艺高强：如《水浒传》中的武松，酒后似醉非醉耍了一套"醉拳"，他头如波浪，拳如流星，脚成碎步，在跌冲摇摆中狠狠地教训了恶霸(bà)蒋门神；《三国演义》里的关羽挥舞大刀，过五关斩六将；《西游记》中的孙悟空手持金箍(gū)棒大闹天宫……这些都是武术在文学作品中的再现。其次是武侠小说，江湖上的武林高

太极拳

手，刀、枪、剑、棍，个个武艺超群。他们是"路见不平一声吼"的侠客，是百姓心中的英雄。另外，中国戏曲中妙不可言的武打表演，则是将武术动作艺术化、唯美化了。

现在，武术已经走出国门，国际间的武术交流非常频繁。到中国学习武术的外国朋友也越来越多，他们更喜欢称武术为"中国功夫"。不少西方人认识中国文化，首先是从中国武术开始的。

生词

wǔ shù 武术	martial art	zhāo shì 招式	movements in martial arts
yōu jiǔ 悠久	long	shuǎ 耍	play
shèng xíng 盛行	prevail	diē 跌	fall
tài jí quán 太极拳	Taijiquan, a kind of traditional Chinese shadow boxing	huī 挥	swing
		chí 持	hold on
yùn dòng 运动	sports	qí cì 其次	secondly
xiàng mù 项目	item; project	xiá kè 侠客	chivalrous man
bù mén 部门	department	guó jì 国际	international
tī 踢	kick	pín fán 频繁	frequent

听写

武术　悠久　盛行　太极拳　项目　部门　踢

跌　挥　持　其次　国际　*耍　频繁

比一比

武 { 武术 / 武器 }　　盛 { 盛大 / 盛行 }　　项 { 项目 / 项链 }

要　　　　耍

需要　　　玩耍

反义词

盛行——过时　　　自卫——进攻

多音字

shèng　　　　　chéng

盛　　　　　　　盛

盛行　　　　　　盛饭

河北民间武术盛行。　我给爷爷奶奶盛饭。
陕西民间盛行剪窗花。　青花瓷碗中盛着饭。

词语运用

盛行

① 近几年人们盛行戴黑框眼镜。

② 有了电影电视之后，戏剧就不太盛行了。

③ 现在的中国，手机支付挺盛行的。

项目

① 在学校运动会上，哥哥参加了游泳项目的比赛。

② 弟弟参加了羽毛球和武术两个项目的训练。

③ 爸爸是公司的项目经理。

词语解释

自卫——受到他人打击，防卫自己不受伤害。

醉拳——模仿醉汉动作的一种传统拳术。

恶霸——指独霸一方、欺压群众的人。

电子邮件的写法（论述文）

1. 格式：发件人：×××

    收件人：×××

    主题：

    正文：

2. 写作要求：观点或事实清楚明白，论述充分，有条理。

3. 文章结构：分4段。

第一段：先讲明自己的观点；

第二段：用"首先"引出第二段，论述第一条原因；

第三段：用"其次"引出第三段，论述第二条原因；

第四段：用"最后"引出第四段，结尾简短、扣题。

中国民俗与民间艺术

范文

发件人：王梅

收件人：小华

邮件主题：暑期活动

小华：

今年暑假我有两个学习机会，一个是去夏令营打工当辅导员，有六个星期；另一个是到我家附近的大学上一门电脑课。我不可能同时做两件事，你觉得我应该选哪项活动呢？请给我一个建议。

谢谢！

王梅

发件人：小华

收件人：王梅

主题：暑假当辅导员很好

王梅：

来信收到。

我觉得你暑假当辅导员是个不错的选择。

首先，你将来并不想当工程师，而是想当老师。当辅导员这个机会让你和孩子们在一起，你可以得到真正的经验。

其次，你可以在夏令营中交很多朋友。谁知道呢，也许在这些小朋友中将来会出一个总统，那多酷啊！

最后，平时学习很累，暑假本来就该休息，和小朋友在一起6周，自己还有两周时间，可以旅行。这样安排应该不错。

小华

> 资料

少林寺

著名的少林寺位于河南嵩(sōng)山,始建于495年(北魏)。少林寺因少林功夫而名扬天下,有"天下功夫出少林,少林功夫甲天下"之说。下图为李连杰出演的电影《少林寺》剧照。

Lesson Nine

Chinese Martial Arts

The martial art is a shining pearl in Chinese traditional culture, also called a national heritage. Originating from and popular among folk people, it has a long history. Shaolinquan and Taijiquan are two famous representatives. Martial arts are not only sports to strengthen the body, but also have a strong humanistic ideology and rich contents such as teaching people to do good, to cultivate the body and mind, and to pursue peace. When students learn martial arts, the teacher will first teach them the traditional virtues of martial arts, understanding the objectives of practicing martial arts are to strengthen the body, to defend oneself, to eliminate evil and to help the weak, to quell a war, and to make peace.

In modern times, The martial art is not a sport only for the young and strong people; with lots of practices suitable for children, the elderly, the weak, and the sick, it is much liked by many. For example, there are teams of martial arts in middle schools and colleges, martial arts gymnastic exercises during class breaks in primary schools nationwide. In schools of physical education, there is a department for the teaching and research of martial arts. With gymnasiums frequently holding various martial arts competitions, martial arts performances abounding in movies and plays, it can be said that the influence of martial art permeates the lives of Chinese people. When one learns martial arts, he is required to stand like a pine, sit like a bell, and walk like the wind; the body should contain and show the essence, energy, and spirit. Most of the martial arts movements are fast and varied. Each move of punching, kicking, and jumping, all manifest the unique oriental beauty of Chinese martial arts.

One form of martial arts, Taijiquan, is well-known by everyone in China. Practicing Taijiquan stresses focus, relaxation, quiet-mindedness, and slow movement. In the morning, many seniors and people of weak physique practice Taijiquan in parks. Their movements are calm, slow and graceful, like floating clouds and flowing water. It's not an easy thing to do one round of Taijiquan. If you do it carefully, after one round, your body will warm up and sweat slightly.

The practice of martial arts has a deep and long-lasting impact on Chinese literature and art. First off, many heroes in classic novels are highly skilled in martial arts. Wu Song in *The Water Margin* is one example. After drinking lots of wine, half drunk and half sober, he played a set of Drunk Fist. His head shaking like waves, fists fast as shooting stars, in crumbling steps, he taught a good lesson to a local bully Jiang Menshen. Guan Yu in *The Three Kingdoms*, wielding a big sword, crossed five hurdles and killed six generals.The Monkey King in *Journey to the West* wreaked havoc in heaven with his golden cudgel in his hands. These are all representation of martial arts in literature. Secondly, there are martial arts fictions, in which the masters of martial arts excel in skills of using swords, guns,

swords, and clubs. In the hearts of common people, they are heroes, who would "roar when they see injustice on the road". In addition, in Chinese operas, the wonderful martial arts performances have transformed the martial arts movement into great artistic beauty.

These days, martial arts have spread outside China. International interactions of martial arts are becoming very frequent. More and more people from foreign countries come to China to learn martial arts, which they prefer to call Chinese Kongfu. For many western people, it is from Chinese martial arts that they get to know about Chinese culture.

第十课

民间艺术——剪纸

天地有大美,在中国农村这片天地间就有一种古老的民间艺术——剪纸,应和着天地之美。剪纸在中国流传很广。当你看到人家门上或窗户上贴着"红双喜"的剪纸,你的心会热起来,那定是有喜庆的婚事。如果家家户户的门窗上都贴了"春"字、"福"字、"五谷丰登"的剪纸,你的心又会浮动起来,因为大人孩子都盼望的春节马上就要来临。别看这小小的剪纸,它轻快地装饰着百姓的生活,带给

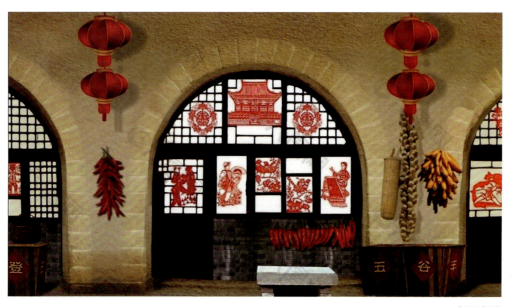

窑洞窗花

人们浓浓的喜庆气氛。

剪纸是怎么产生的呢？传说，有一位姓陈的穷书生，随手在纸上写了一个"福"字，妻子把它撕了出来，这就是剪纸的起源。传说不足为凭，考古发现，剪纸早在1,500年前（南北朝）就有了。

古时，在农村，人们的窗户多是纸糊的，白白的窗户纸很单调，没有生气。有了剪子，有了纸，心灵手巧的女子便把自己心中喜欢的东西剪出来。剪个红色的四喜娃娃或剪一只漂亮的蝴蝶，贴在窗户上作为窗

花，顿时平凡的窗户便有了生气。剪子不够用，有时候也用刀子刻。过去在农村，女孩子都学习剪纸。人们认为剪花好的女人心灵手巧。

千百年来，中国人喜爱剪纸。剪着剪着，图案越来越美，种类也越来越多：有窗花、灯花、吉祥字、人物、风景、故事……剪纸有单色的，也有彩色的，形成了不同的风格。其中陕西的窗花、河北蔚(yù)县的戏剧人物、扬州剪纸都很有名。中国人生生用一把剪子和一张纸，剪出了他们的生活趣味，剪出对吉祥幸福的

向往。熟练的剪纸艺人就像变魔术一样,一张红纸在他们手上左叠右叠,用剪刀轻轻剪几下,打开一看,就是一幅漂亮的图画。剪纸的图案,带有浓重的乡土气息,纯朴精美。而今,人们除了过年过节用剪纸作装饰,平时也把它作为精美的艺术品收藏。

目前中国剪纸已被列入世界文化遗产。

北京大学西门剪纸

第十课

生词

jiǎn zhǐ 剪纸	paper-cut	xīn líng shǒu qiǎo 心灵手巧	smart and deft
wǔ gǔ fēng dēng 五谷丰登	abundant harvest of five staples	tú àn 图案	pattern, design
		shú liàn 熟练	skillful
lái lín 来临	coming	yì rén 艺人	craftsman
zhuāng shì 装饰	decorate	mó shù 魔术	magic
hú 糊	paste, glue	xiāng tǔ qì xī 乡土气息	country flavor
dān diào 单调	monotonous	chún pǔ 纯朴	simple, unsophisticated
píng fán 平凡	ordinary		

听写

剪纸　五谷丰登　来临　糊　单调　平凡　心灵手巧

图案　熟练　魔术　乡土气息　＊纯朴

比一比

登 { 登山 / 登录 / 登记 }　　临 { 来临 / 临走 / 光临 }　　遗 { 遗产 / 遗憾 / 遗址 }

反义词

来临——离开　　　　单调——丰富

量词

"叠"也可以作量词：

一（叠）纸　　　　一（叠）钱

吉祥字剪纸

寿

福　年年有余

福　禄　寿　喜　恭喜发财

词语运用

来临

① 春节即将来临，家家户户都贴上了春联。

② 考试即将来临，学生们都紧张地复习功课。

顿时

① 老师走进教室，全班顿时安静下来。

② 梅兰芳先生演完京剧，全场顿时掌声雷动。

③ 小弟弟听说不带他去玩儿，顿时大哭起来。

向往

① 世界人民都向往和平。

② 人们向往更美好的生活。

中国民俗与民间艺术

词语解释

不足为凭——不能作为凭证或根据。

生气——课文里指有活力。

向往——希望达到或得到。

阅读

扬州剪纸

扬州剪纸,是中国南方剪纸艺术的代表之一。早在唐宋时期,扬州就有剪纸报春的习俗。一到立春之日,人们就剪花鸟、蝴蝶;也剪纸马、纸钱用于清明扫墓。

扬州的剪纸艺术,离不开扬州的好纸。那时的扬州,已可以生产大量高品质的贡纸。明清时期,作为丝绸之乡的扬州,百姓服饰以绣(xiù)花为美,而绣花时要用剪纸为底样。由此,扬州剪纸便从刺绣花样中走了出来。扬州剪纸多为一色,线条精致流畅(chàng),艺人用剪刀代替(tì)了毛笔,剪出了中国的"白描画",让人惊叹!

河北蔚县剪纸

河北蔚县剪纸已有600多年历史了，风格独特，主要有三点：

一是剪纸的主要工具，已由"剪子"变为"刻刀"。剪纸是用刻刀"刻"出来的。

二是剪纸内容丰富，除了花鸟虫鱼之外，还有传说故事、戏曲人物等。仅蔚县剪纸的戏曲人物，就有上千个。

三是蔚县剪纸注重形象的传神，色彩浓艳鲜明、喜气洋洋，表现出北方农民奔放热烈的生活情趣。

中国民俗与民间艺术

资料

中国剪纸欣赏

蒙古族姑娘

《红楼梦》

Lesson Ten

Folk Art: Paper Cutting

Under the sky, there is great beauty on the earth. In the vast land of Chinese countryside, there is a form of ancient folk art—paper cutting. The art of paper cutting is widely spread in China. When you see the paper cuts of "red double joy" on the doors and windows of a house, your heart will feel warm, for it is certain that there must be a joyful wedding. If on the doors and windows of every households there are paper cuts of "spring" "bliss" and "abundant harvest of five staples", your heart will again leap, because the Spring Festival yearned by both adults and children will soon come. Don't look down on the small pieces of paper cutting, for they very conveniently adorn the life of ordinary people and bring to people much joyful atmosphere on holidays.

How did paper cutting come into being? Legend goes that after a poor scholar with the family name of Chen casually wrote the character of "Bliss" in a piece of paper, his wife tore the used paper but kept the character, thus starting paper cutting. The folklore cannot be taken as evidence though. According to archeology findings, paper cutting appeared as early as 1,500 years ago (in the period of South and North Dynasty).

In the old times, in the countryside, people's windows were mostly made by paper coverings. The white window paper was monotonous and lifeless. With a pair of scissors and paper, clever women with deft fingers could cut out whatever they liked. They cut out a red baby with four blessings or a beautiful butterfly, glued them on the window, and the ordinary windows were instantly enlivened by the decorations. Sometimes scissors were not enough, so a knife could do as well. In the past, in countryside, each girl needed to learn paper cutting. People considered women good at paper cutting smart and deft.

For hundreds and thousands of years, Chinese people have loved paper cutting. As time goes by, the designs become more and more beautiful, and there are more and more varieties. window flowers, lamp flowers, auspicious Chinese characters, figures, sceneries, and stories. There are single colored paper cuttings and colorful paper cuttings, forming different styles. Window flowers in Shaanxi, opera figures in Yu County, Hebei Province, and paper cuttings in Yangzhou are all famous representatives. Simply by using a pair of scissors and a piece of paper, Chinese people cut out their life interest, their longing for auspiciousness and happiness.

Skillful craftsmen of paper cutting is like a magician. By folding a piece of red paper several times and then lightly cutting it, they turn the paper into a beautiful picture after unfolding it. The design of paper cutting has a strong rustic characteristic, simple but exquisite. Nowadays, besides using the paper cuttings as decorations on festivals, people also collect paper cuttings as beautiful artwork in normal time.

Chinese paper cutting has now been listed as a World Cultural Heritage.

Yangzhou Paper Cutting

Yangzhou paper cutting is one of the representatives of the paper cutting art in South China. In as early as the Tang and Song Dynasty, there was the custom of paper cutting in Yangzhou to herald the coming of spring. On the day of Lichun(Start of Spring), people cut out flowers, birds, and butterflies; also on Qingming(Pure Brightness), they cut out paper horses and paper money for sweeping tombs.

The art of paper cutting in Yangzhou is inseparable from the good paper in Yangzhou. At that time, Yangzhou could mass produce high-quality paper for the use of the royal family. In Ming and Qing Dynasty, ordinary people in Yangzhou, as one of the hometowns of silk, regarded clothing with embroidery as beautiful. As silk embroidery had to use paper cutting as sample pattern, the paper cutting in Yangzhou found its way out of embroidery samples. Most of Yangzhou paper cutting has a single color with exquisite and smooth lines. Using scissors in place of a brush, the craftsmen cut out the Chinese Line Drawings. How amazing!

Paper Cutting in Yu County, Hebei Province

The paper cutting in Yu County, Hebei, has a history of over 600 years. The style in this place is very unique, shown in three aspects:

First, the main tool for paper cutting has changed from the scissor to the carving knife. The paper cutting is carved out by the carving knife.

Second, the content of the paper cutting is very rich. Besides flowers, birds, insects, and fish, there are also legend stories, opera characters, etc.. The number of opera characters alone in paper cutting in Yu County has reached more than one thousand.

Third, the paper cutting in Yu County pays special attention to conveying the spirit of characters. The colors are bold and bright, full of joy, reflecting the effusiveness and enthusiasm towards life of the farmers in North China.

生字表（简）

1. 俗(sú) 聆(líng) 暑(shǔ) 霜(shuāng) 谚(yàn) 耘(yún) 诀(jué) 统(tǒng) 朗(lǎng) 祭(jì) 饮(yǐn) 酱(jiàng)
拌(bàn) 魂(hún) 牧(mù) 遗(yí)

2. 挤(jǐ) 浓(nóng) 氛(fēn) 贴(tiē) 聚(jù) 饺(jiǎo) 夕(xī) 聊(liáo) 戚(qī) 拜(bài) 祥(xiáng) 剪(jiǎn)
裕(yù) 鞭(biān) 炮(pào)

3. 雅(yǎ) 厢(xiāng) 辈(bèi) 顾(gù) 乘(chéng) 逸(yì) 窑(yáo) 灵(líng) 防(fáng) 径(jìng) 框(kuàng) 毡(zhān)
毯(tǎn)

4. 寺(sì) 矩(jǔ) 叠(dié) 托(tuō) 檐(yán) 榫(sǔn) 卯(mǎo) 勾(gōu) 吨(dūn) 誉(yù) 庄(zhuāng) 严(yán)
翘(qiào) 紫(zǐ) 禁(jìn) 碧(bì) 绘(huì) 描(miáo) 湮(yān)

5. 腔(qiāng) 妆(zhuāng) 虚(xū) 拟(nǐ) 桨(jiǎng) 丑(chǒu) 豪(háo) 幽(yōu) 谱(pǔ) 忠(zhōng) 奸(jiān) 诈(zhà)
饰(shì) 卉(huì) 唯(wéi) 瘾(yǐn) 粹(cuì)

6. 柴(chái) 醋(cù) 杯(bēi) 爽(shuǎng) 饮(yǐn) 专(zhuān) 咬(yǎo) 肿(zhǒng) 疮(chuāng) 泻(xiè) 醇(jiào) 艳(yàn)
售(shòu) 橙(chéng)

7. 俱(jù) 辣(là) 葱(cōng) 蒸(zhēng) 腐(fǔ) 聚(jù) 招(zhāo) 挺(tǐng) 馅(xiàn) 遗(yí) 憾(hàn) 酥(sū) 嫩(nèn)
抹(mǒ) 顾(gù) 饱(bǎo) 馨(xīn) 尊(zūn)

中国民俗与民间艺术

8. 匾(biǎn) 额(é) 踪(zōng) 匀(yún) 汁(zhī) 宣(xuān) 虚(xū) 抽(chōu) 凭(píng) 宛(wǎn) 审(shěn) 局(jú) 隶(lì)
   楷(kǎi) 牌(pái) 砚(yàn)

9. 盛(shèng) 拳(quán) 项(xiàng) 踢(tī) 招(zhāo) 耍(shuǎ) 跌(diē) 挥(huī) 持(chí) 侠(xiá) 频(pín)

10. 登(dēng) 临(lín) 巧(qiǎo) 案(àn) 魔(mó) 纯(chún) 朴(pǔ)

共计 146 个生字　累计 1789 个生字

生字表（繁）

1. 俗(sú) 聆(líng) 暑(shǔ) 霜(shuāng) 諺(yàn) 耘(yún) 訣(jué) 統(tǒng) 朗(lǎng) 祭(jì) 飲(yǐn) 醬(jiàng)
拌(bàn) 魂(hún) 牧(mù) 遺(yí)

2. 擠(jǐ) 濃(nóng) 氛(fēn) 貼(tiē) 聚(jù) 餃(jiǎo) 夕(xī) 聊(liáo) 戚(qī) 拜(bài) 祥(xiáng) 剪(jiǎn)
裕(yù) 鞭(biān) 炮(pào)

3. 雅(yǎ) 廂(xiāng) 輩(bèi) 顧(gù) 乘(chéng) 逸(yì) 窯(yáo) 靈(líng) 防(fáng) 徑(jìng) 框(kuàng) 氈(zhān)
毯(tǎn)

4. 寺(sì) 矩(jǔ) 疊(dié) 托(tuō) 檐(yán) 榫(sǔn) 卯(mǎo) 勾(gōu) 噸(dūn) 譽(yù) 莊(zhuāng) 嚴(yán)
翹(qiào) 紫(zǐ) 禁(jìn) 碧(bì) 繪(huì) 描(miáo) 湮(yān)

5. 腔(qiāng) 妝(zhuāng) 虛(xū) 擬(nǐ) 漿(jiāng) 醜(chǒu) 豪(háo) 幽(yōu) 譜(pǔ) 忠(zhōng) 奸(jiān) 詐(zhà)
飾(shì) 卉(huì) 唯(wéi) 癮(yǐn) 粹(cuì)

6. 柴(chái) 醋(cù) 杯(bēi) 爽(shuǎng) 飲(yǐn) 專(zhuān) 咬(yǎo) 腫(zhǒng) 瘡(chuāng) 瀉(xiè) 酵(jiào) 艷(yàn)
售(shòu) 橙(chéng)

7. 俱(jù) 辣(là) 蔥(cōng) 蒸(zhēng) 腐(fǔ) 聚(jù) 招(zhāo) 挺(tǐng) 餡(xiàn) 遺(yí) 憾(hàn) 酥(sū) 嫩(nèn)
抹(mǒ) 顧(gù) 飽(bǎo) 馨(xīn) 尊(zūn)

8. 匾(biǎn) 額(é) 踪(zōng) 勻(yún) 汁(zhī) 宣(xuān) 虛(xū) 抽(chōu) 憑(píng) 宛(wǎn) 審(shěn) 局(jú) 隸(lì)
楷(kǎi) 牌(pái) 硯(yàn)

9. 盛(shèng) 拳(quán) 項(xiàng) 踢(tī) 招(zhāo) 耍(shuǎ) 跌(diē) 揮(huī) 持(chí) 俠(xiá) 頻(pín)

10. 登(dēng) 臨(lín) 巧(qiǎo) 案(àn) 魔(mó) 純(chún) 樸(pǔ)

共計 146 個生字　纍計 1789 個生字

生词表（简）

1. 节气(jié qì) 民俗(mín sú) 聆听(líng tīng) 暑(shǔ) 霜(shuāng) 粮食(liáng shi) 农谚(nóng yàn) 耘(yún) 口诀(kǒu jué)
传统(chuán tǒng) 朗(lǎng) 扫墓(sǎo mù) 祭祖(jì zǔ) 饮食(yǐn shí) 酱(jiàng) 拌(bàn) 习俗(xí sú) 魂(hún) 牧童(mù tóng)
遗产(yí chǎn)

2. 喜庆(xǐ qìng) 挤满(jǐ mǎn) 浓(nóng) 气氛(qì fēn) 贴(tiē) 团聚(tuán jù) 饺子(jiǎo zi) 除夕(chú xī) 聊天(liáo tiān)
亲戚(qīn qi) 拜年(bài nián) 恭喜(gōng xǐ) 吉祥(jí xiáng) 祝福(zhù fú) 游行(yóu xíng) 剪(jiǎn) 富裕(fù yù) 鞭炮(biān pào)

3. 民居(mín jū) 优雅(yōu yǎ) 厢房(xiāng fáng) 庭院(tíng yuàn) 封闭(fēng bì) 长辈(zhǎng bèi) 照顾(zhào gù) 乘凉(chéng liáng)
安逸(ān yì) 窑洞(yáo dòng) 灵气(líng qì) 防火(fáng huǒ) 直径(zhí jìng) 框架(kuàng jià) 毡(zhān) 挂毯(guà tǎn)

4. 寺庙(sì miào) 斗拱(dǒu gǒng) 构件(gòu jiàn) 矩形(jǔ xíng) 叠(dié) 托(tuō) 檐(yán) 榫卯(sǔn mǎo) 勾连(gōu lián) 吨(dūn)
荣誉(róng yù) 稳固(wěn gù) 庄严(zhuāng yán) 微（翘）(wēi qiào) 紫禁城(zǐ jìn chéng) 金碧辉煌(jīn bì huī huáng) 系统(xì tǒng)
测绘(cè huì) 顿时(dùn shí) 白描(bái miáo) 湮没(yān mò)

5. 唱腔(chàng qiāng) 化妆(huà zhuāng) 曲调(qǔ diào) 表现(biǎo xiàn) 虚拟(xū nǐ) 桨(jiǎng) 演员(yǎn yuán) 丑(chǒu) 性格(xìng gé)
豪放(háo fàng) 幽默(yōu mò) 脸谱(liǎn pǔ) 忠勇(zhōng yǒng) 奸诈(jiān zhà) 服饰(fú shì) 花卉(huā huì) 唯美(wéi měi) 过瘾(guò yǐn)
国粹(guó cuì)

中国民俗与民间艺术

6. 柴 醋 杯 爽 饮料 专家 划破 叮咬 红肿
   生疮 上吐下泻 发酵 红艳 销售 橙 讲究

7. 俱全 辣 葱 蒸 豆腐 聚会 招待 挺 馅儿
   遗憾 酥 嫩 抹 顾客 饱 温馨 尊重

8. 匾额 无影无踪 匀称 墨汁 宣纸 虚实 抽象 意境
   凭空 宛然 审美 布局 隶书 楷书 名牌 砚台

9. 武术 悠久 盛行 太极拳 运动 项目 部门 踢
   招式 耍 跌 挥 持 其次 侠客 国际 频繁

10. 剪纸 五谷丰登 来临 装饰 糊 单调 平凡
    心灵手巧 图案 熟练 艺人 魔术 乡土气息
    纯朴

共计 175 个生词

生词表（繁）

1. 節氣 民俗 聆聽 暑 霜 糧食 農諺 耘 口訣
   傳統 朗 掃墓 祭祖 飲食 醬 拌 習俗 魂 牧童
   遺產

2. 喜慶 擠滿 濃 氣氛 貼 團聚 餃子 除夕 聊天
   親戚 拜年 恭喜 吉祥 祝福 遊行 剪 富裕 鞭炮

3. 民居 優雅 廂房 庭院 封閉 長輩 照顧 乘涼
   安逸 窯洞 靈氣 防火 直徑 框架 氈 挂毯

4. 寺廟 斗拱 構件 矩形 疊 托 檐 榫卯 勾連 頓
   榮譽 穩固 莊嚴 微（翹） 紫禁城 金碧輝煌 系統
   測繪 頓時 白描 湮沒

5. 唱腔 化妝 曲調 表現 虛擬 槳 演員 丑 性格
   豪放 幽默 臉譜 忠勇 奸詐 服飾 花卉 唯美 過癮
   國粹

中国民俗与民间艺术

6. 柴(chái) 醋(cù) 杯(bēi) 爽(shuǎng) 飲料(yǐn liào) 專家(zhuān jiā) 劃破(huá pò) 叮咬(dīng yǎo) 紅腫(hóng zhǒng) 生瘡(shēng chuāng) 上吐下瀉(shàng tù xià xiè) 發酵(fā jiào) 紅艷(hóng yàn) 銷售(xiāo shòu) 橙(chéng) 講究(jiǎng jiu)

7. 俱全(jù quán) 辣(là) 蔥(cōng) 蒸(zhēng) 豆腐(dòu fu) 聚會(jù huì) 招待(zhāo dài) 挺(tǐng) 餡兒(xiànr) 遺憾(yí hàn) 酥(sū) 嫩(nèn) 抹(mǒ) 顧客(gù kè) 飽(bǎo) 溫馨(wēn xīn) 尊重(zūn zhòng)

8. 匾額(biǎn é) 無影無踪(wú yǐng wú zōng) 勻稱(yún chèn) 墨汁(mò zhī) 宣紙(xuān zhǐ) 虛實(xū shí) 抽象(chōu xiàng) 意境(yì jìng) 憑空(píng kōng) 宛然(wǎn rán) 審美(shěn měi) 佈局(bù jú) 隸書(lì shū) 楷書(kǎi shū) 名牌(míng pái) 硯臺(yàn tai)

9. 武術(wǔ shù) 悠久(yōu jiǔ) 盛行(shèng xíng) 太極拳(tài jí quán) 運動(yùn dòng) 項目(xiàng mù) 部門(bù mén) 踢(tī) 招式(zhāo shì) 耍(shuǎ) 跌(diē) 揮(huī) 持(chí) 其次(qí cì) 俠客(xiá kè) 國際(guó jì) 頻繁(pín fán)

10. 剪紙(jiǎn zhǐ) 五谷豐登(wǔ gǔ fēng dēng) 來臨(lái lín) 裝飾(zhuāng shì) 糊(hú) 單調(dān diào) 平凡(píng fán) 心靈手巧(xīn líng shǒu qiǎo) 圖案(tú àn) 熟練(shú liàn) 藝人(yì rén) 魔術(mó shù) 鄉土氣息(xiāng tǔ qì xī) 純樸(chún pǔ)

共計 175 個生詞

附录

"新双双中文教材"写作练习（1—11册）

课文正式教授写作内容

内容	出处	建议学习年级
1. 课文缩写	第4册 "猴子捞月亮"	3—4年级
2. 日记	第5册 "妈妈教我写日记"	4—5年级
3. 叙事文	第5册 "参观兵马俑"	4—5年级
4. 看图写故事	第6册《中国成语故事》"塞翁失马"	5—6年级
5. 城市介绍	第7册《中国地理常识》"著名城市"	5—6年级
6. 书信	第8册《中国古代故事》"七步诗"	5—6年级
7. 写人	第9册《中国神话传说》"嫦娥奔月"	6—7年级
8. 电子邮件的写法（论述文）	第11册《中国民俗与民间艺术》"中国武术"	7—8年级

辅助写作练习

内容	出处	建议学习年级
1. 读书笔记	亲子阅读，每周家庭读书、写作	2—6年级
2. 观察记录	第4册 写"养蚕报告"	3—4年级
3. 创作	写简单的故事和想法	4年级以上

新双双中文教材 11

New Chinese Language and Culture Course

中国民俗与民间艺术
Chinese Folklore and Folk Art

练习本 单课

[美] 王双双 编著

北京大学出版社

目 录

第一课　二十四节气 …………………………………… 1

第三课　独特的民居 …………………………………… 7

第五课　京剧 …………………………………………… 12

第七课　中国菜 ………………………………………… 18

第九课　中国武术 ……………………………………… 24

第一课
二十四节气

一 写生词

暑					
霜					
耘					
朗					
酱					
拌					
魂					
节	气				
民	俗				
聆	听				

粮	食				
农	谚				
口	诀				
传	统				
扫	墓				
祭	祖				
饮	食				
习	俗				
牧	童				
遗	产				

二 下列汉字是由哪些部分组成的

第一课 二十四节气

三 组词

暑{_____ 俗{_____ 饮{_____ 童{_____

四 选字组词

（祭 蔡）祖　　（拌 绊）倒　　夏（耘 云）

（祭 蔡）伦　　（拌 绊）菜　　白（耘 云）

五 给下面的词语加拼音

聆听 _____　　　　农耕 _____

六 选择填空

1. 立春，"立"意为_____，春季开始了。

2. 春分，"分"意为平分。这天，白天和黑夜_____。

3. 雨水，开始下雨，不再_____了。

第一课
二十四节气

4. 惊蛰，"蛰"意为藏，春雷响，_____了冬眠的虫子。

5. 谷雨，南方开始_____，谷雨这天总要喝点儿新茶。

七 解释下列节气的意思

立夏，这个节气的意思是_____。

大暑，这个节气的意思是_____。

大寒，这个节气的意思是_____。

八 判断对错

1. 中国人的衣食住行从来没离开过二十四节气。　　___对___错

2. 二十四节气还与安排农事息息相关。　　___对___错

3. "清明前后，种瓜点豆"是节气农谚。　　___对___错

4. 清明节是扫墓祭祖的节日。　　___对___错

5. 冬至这天吃饺子，夏至这天吃包子。　　___对___错

6. 小满是节气，也是祭蚕神的节日。　　___对___错

7. 二十四节气现在已成为世界非物质文化遗产了。　　___对___错

第一课
二十四节气

☆ ---------- ☆ ---------- ☆

九 将方框中的词语与适当的解释连线

息息相关	家家户户都知道。
扫墓祭祖	指耕地、除草、防病虫害等。
家喻户晓	彼此连呼吸都互相关联。
农事	清扫墓地，纪念祖先亲人。

十 读诗歌找出节气名，写在横线上（共24个）

立春雨水渐，惊蛰虫不眠，_____ _____ _____

春分近清明，采茶谷雨前；_____ _____ _____

立夏小满足，芒种大开镰(lián)，_____ _____ _____

夏至才小暑，大暑三伏天；_____ _____ _____

立秋处暑去，白露南飞雁，_____ _____ _____

秋分寒露至，霜降红叶染；_____ _____ _____

立冬小雪飘，大雪兆(zhào)丰年，_____ _____ _____

冬至数九日，小寒又大寒。_____ _____ _____

4

第一课 二十四节气

十一 将下列图和印章上的字写出来

_____   _____   _____   _____

十二 谜语和游戏

- 谜语：春雷一声响，万物齐生长。（打一节气名）

谜底是_____。

- 解释：春分、秋分，日夜对半分。

意思是_____。

- 下列三个词语中，哪个是节气，请圈出

  中秋   立秋   春秋

- 排出六个节气的先后顺序

  立冬 小雪 大寒 大雪 冬至 小寒

  1. _____   2. _____   3. _____

  4. _____   5. _____   6. _____

第一课 二十四节气

十三　为二十四节气设计一张海报

提示：气温、动物、植物、降水、农事等。

十四　读课文两遍

第三课 独特的民居

一 写生词

毡					
民	居				
优	雅				
厢	房				
庭	院				
封	闭				
长	辈				
照	顾				

乘	凉				
安	逸				
窑	洞				
灵	气				
防	火				
直	径				
框	架				
挂	毯				

二 下列汉字是由哪些部分组成的

辈 ⟶ ☐ + ☐   毡 ⟶ ☐ + ☐

氛 ⟶ ☐ + ☐   毯 ⟶ ☐ + ☐

闭 ⟶ ☐ + ☐   厢 ⟶ ☐ + ☐

第三课 独特的民居

三 组词

居民　车厢　信封　家庭

居 { _____
封 { _____

厢 { _____
庭 { _____

四 选字组词

（传　专）统　　（防　方）火　　车（厢　相）

（传　专）家　　（防　方）法　　互（厢　相）

五 写出反义词

紧张　低俗　晚辈　新潮　普通　公开

安逸—_____　　神秘—_____　　长辈—_____

优雅—_____　　独特—_____　　传统—_____

六 给下面的词语加拼音

| 庭院 | _____ | 窑洞 | _____ | 安逸 | _____ |

第三课 独特的民居

七 将方框中的词语与适当的解释连线

北京四合院	东西南北四边的房子围起来的院落。
窑洞	外墙多用白色，有高高的马头墙。
江南民居	是圆形的，一种容易搬动的"房子"。
蒙古包	好处是省工省料，住起来冬暖夏凉。

八 选词填空

1. 北京最有代表性的民居是_____。

2. 在黄土高原上，老百姓创造了一种民居叫_____。

3. 水是南方民居独特的_____。

4. 江南民居建筑中，高高的马头墙是用来_____的。

5. 蒙古包是_____的，面积不大，直径4～6米。

6. 蒙古包是用木条编成_____，外边再包上羊毛毡子。

九 根据课文判断对错

1. 在四合院中，一般长辈住正房，晚辈住厢房。　　___对___错

第三课 独特的民居

2. 四合院开着大门是一个封闭的空间。　　　　　___对___错

3. 窑洞一般是在黄土坡上直接往里挖。　　　　　___对___错

4. 窑洞虽然冬暖夏凉，但是有一点儿潮湿。　　　___对___错

5. 二层的江南民居，底层是木结构，上层是砖结构。___对___错

6. 江南民居外墙是白色，瓦是黑色，很素雅。　　　___对___错

7. 蒙古包顶部有圆形天窗，用来采光和通风。　　　___对___错

8. 蒙古包是方形的，面积很大。　　　　　　　　　___对___错

十　造句

传统_____

十一　谜语　猜民居，请将谜底写在"_____"

| 青砖黛瓦 马头墙 | 山坡挖洞 冬暖夏凉 |

_____　　　　　　　　　_____

第三课
独特的民居

☆ ---------- ☆ ---------- ☆

| 圆形毡房
 方便搬家 | | 四面房屋
 围着庭院 |

_____   _____

十二 阅读作业

下面是中式马头墙的式样，你喜欢哪一种？请画出

十三 读课文两遍

第五课 京剧

一 写生词

桨						幽	默				
丑						脸	谱				
唱	腔					忠	勇				
化	妆					奸	诈				
曲	调					服	饰				
表	现					花	卉				
虚	拟					唯	美				
演	员					过	瘾				
性	格					国	粹				
豪	放										

二 下列汉字是由哪些部分组成的

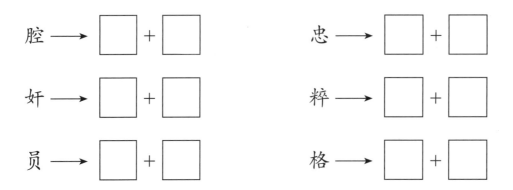

第五课 京剧

三 组词

乐谱　虚心　调皮　装饰

谱 ｛ _____ _____ ｝　　虚 ｛ _____ _____ ｝

饰 ｛ _____ _____ ｝　　调 ｛ _____ _____ ｝

四 选字组词

唱（腔　空）　　虚（以　拟）　　过（瘾　急）

航（腔　空）　　可（以　拟）　　着（瘾　急）

五 写出反义词

真实　老实　真实　单调

幽默—_____　　　　　夸张—_____

虚拟—_____　　　　　奸诈—_____

六 给下面的词语加拼音

虚拟 _____　　　过瘾 _____　　　国粹 _____

第五课 京剧

七 将方框中的词语与适当的解释连线

"生"的行当　　　扮演女人，分青衣、花旦、武旦和老旦。

"旦"的行当　　　扮演性格豪放的男人，要画脸谱，也叫花脸。

"净"的行当　　　扮演男人，分老生、小生和武生。

"丑"的行当　　　扮演幽默机智或狡猾的男人。

八 选词填空

1. 京剧_____在北京，有200多年历史了。

2. 京剧不像歌剧，只唱歌不_____。

3. 京剧的唱腔非常_____，表现力强。

4. 京剧的_____表演动作，更是一绝。

5. 京剧的_____可说是绚丽多彩。

6. 京剧是中国的_____。

九 根据课文判断对错

1. 京剧艺术包括"唱、念、做、打"四个方面的表演。____对____错

第五课 京剧

2. 京剧的演员分生、旦、净、丑四个行当。　　　　___对___错

3. 京剧的虚拟表演动作，演员需要道具才能表演。　___对___错

4. 京剧脸谱用夸张的色彩图案表现人物品德性格。　___对___错

5. 京剧有的武生身穿丝袍，背后插着四面小旗子。　___对___错

6. 京剧大师梅兰芳是著名的青衣演员。　　　　　　___对___错

十 造句

既……又……_____

十一 写出下图京剧的行当名称

_____　_____　_____　_____

第五课 京 剧

十二 写出下列脸谱代表的人物，并给空白脸谱上色

> 忠勇的人物
> 幽默机智或狡猾的人物
> 奸诈的人物

_____   _____   _____

十三 创意作业"走进京剧"

1. 请给京剧做一张宣传海报，要求：图文并茂

第五课 京　剧

2. 先看京剧《三岔口》或《拾玉镯》，再写出你印象最深的是什么

比如：唱腔、音乐、脸谱、武打、服装、舞蹈等方面

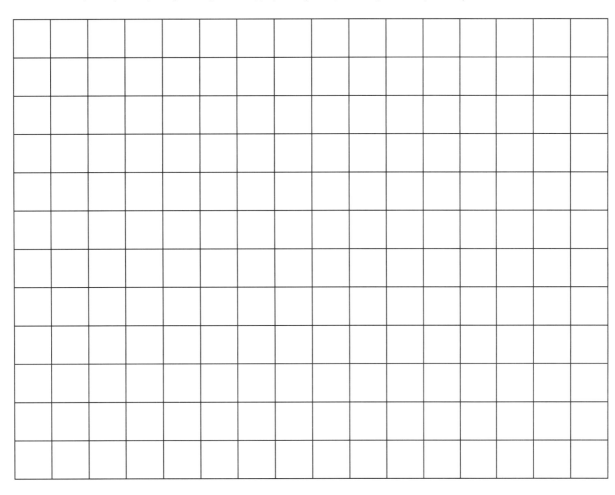

十四　熟读课文两遍

第七课 中国菜

一 写生词

辣					
葱					
蒸					
挺					
酥					
嫩					
抹					
饱					
俱	全				

豆	腐				
聚	会				
招	待				
馅	儿				
遗	憾				
顾	客				
温	馨				
尊	重				

二 组词

等待　聚会　餐馆　顾客

聚 { ____ / ____ }

顾 { ____ / ____ }

餐 { ____ / ____ }

待 { ____ / ____ }

第七课 中国菜

三 选字组词

（并 饼）干　　餐（馆 官）　　遗（憾 感）

（并 饼）且　　高（馆 官）　　情（憾 感）

四 写出反义词

圆满　散　饿　简单

麻烦—_____　　　　饱—_____

遗憾—_____　　　　聚—_____

五 给下面的词语加拼音

餐馆 _____　　聚会 _____　　温馨 _____

六 将方框中的词语与适当的解释连线

南方人　　北方人　　四川人　　广东人

爱吃麻辣　　爱吃咸　　爱吃甜　　爱吃鲜

第七课 中国菜

七 将方框里的词句与适当的解释连线

> 好吃不过饺子
>
> 有钱没钱，吃饺子过年
>
> 千家万户
>
> 五花八门

穷人过年也得吃一顿饺子。

比喻家家户户。

比喻花样多。

饺子是最好吃的食品。

八 选择填空

1. 由于中国地域辽阔，人们的_____也不相同。

2. 四川菜是_____味的。

3. 饺子是中国百姓千家万户的传统_____。

4. 不到长城非好汉，不吃烤鸭真_____。

5. 著名的"狗不理"包子店，在中国_____。

6. 中国人吃饭，是家人围坐，互相夹菜，边吃边聊，很_____。

九 根据课文判断对错

1. 中国地域辽阔，各地气候物产不同，有许多风味菜。____对____错

第七课 中国菜

2. 广东人吃麻辣，四川人吃鲜。　　　　　　　　　　___对___错

3. 北京全聚德烤鸭店是个老字号。　　　　　　　　　___对___错

4. 吃完北京烤鸭的客人都很满意，还想再来。　　　　___对___错

5. 天津著名的"狗不理"包子店原来叫德聚号。　　　___对___错

6. 中国人吃饭，还是家人团聚和交友的一部分。　　　___对___错

十 看图写菜名：

（北京烤鸭　羊肉串　饺子　麻婆豆腐　小笼包　清蒸鱼）

_____　　_____　　_____

_____　　_____　　_____

第七课 中国菜

十一 造句

顾不上 _____

遗憾 _____

十二 在下文中填上合适的菜名

（北京烤鸭　小笼包　羊肉串　清蒸鱼　饺子　麻婆豆腐）

爸爸是广东人，他最爱吃的菜是_____。妈妈是北京人，她更喜欢吃_____和_____。弟弟喜欢上海风味小吃_____；可是吃了新疆风味小吃_____，他说吃得也很过瘾！姐姐去四川工作，她学会了做四川菜_____。

十三 做一张中国美食地图，在地图上写出各地的美食

提示：中国各地区食品的不同风味，有名的风味菜（食品）最好是你知道的吃过的。

如：饺子、北京烤鸭、天津狗不理包子、四川麻婆豆腐、广东清蒸鱼、山东葱烧海参、上海小笼包、新疆羊肉串等。

第七课
中国菜

中国地图

十四　写一写"我印象最深的中国食品是……"

提示：为什么这种食品给你留下印象？好吃/不好吃/味道奇怪，好看，样子、图案、色彩等，在哪里看到、吃到的，有什么故事告诉我们。

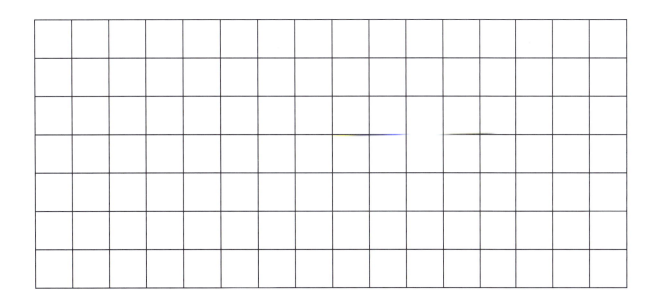

十五　熟读课文两遍

第九课 中国武术

一 写生词

踢						项	目				
耍						部	门				
跌						招	式				
挥						其	次				
持						侠	客				
武	术					国	际				
悠	久					频	繁				
盛	行					太	极	拳			
运	动										

二 下列汉字是由哪些部分组成的

国 → ☐ + ☐   妙 → ☐ + ☐

解 → ☐ + ☐ + ☐   项 → ☐ + ☐

第九课 中国武术

☆ ---------- ☆ ---------- ☆

三 组词

盛大　项链　微笑　一望无际

际 { _____
　　_____ }

项 { _____
　　_____ }

盛 { _____
　　_____ }

微 { _____
　　_____ }

四 选字组词

重（要　耍）　　招（式　试）　　（建　健）康

玩（要　耍）　　考（式　试）　　（建　健）筑

五 写出反义词

进攻　过时

盛行—_____　　　自卫—_____

六 给下面的字词加拼音

盛行 _____　　　盛饭 _____

挥 _____　　　军 _____

第九课 中国武术

七 将方框里的字词和适当的解释连线

妙不可言	武术道德：强身、自卫、除恶助弱等。
首先	好到无法用语言形容。
修身养性	通过自我反省，使身心达到完美的境界。
武德	最先。

八 选择填空

基础　国粹　缓慢　首先　太极拳

1. 武术是中国传统文化中的一颗明珠，被称为_____。

2. 中国老年或体弱多病的人，很喜爱_____。

3. 太极拳动作柔和_____，如行云流水。

4. 戏曲中的武打表演，也是以武术为_____发展出来的。

5. 许多西方人认识中国文化，_____是从中国武术开始的。

九 根据课文判断对错

1. 武术的历史很悠久。　　　　　　　　　　____对____错

2. 武德中重要的是明白习武的目的。　　　　____对____错

第九课 中国武术

3. 中国的许多中学、大学里有武术队。　　　　　　　___对___错

4. 武术对中国文学艺术影响不大。　　　　　　　　　___对___错

5. 现在国际上武术交流活动不少。　　　　　　　　　___对___错

十　造句

首先……其次……_____

十一　论述文写作：写回复邮件

发件人：玛丽

收件人：李林

邮件主题：住宿问题

李林：

　　好消息！我得到了一个到中国去学习汉语和文化的机会。昨天我收到了学校的来信，告诉我可以选择住在学校宿舍，是双人房，或者是在一个中国家庭居住。那个家庭有一个跟我年岁差不多的孩子。你觉得我应该怎样选择？应该从哪些方面考虑？谢谢。

玛丽

第九课
中国武术

回信

十二 熟读课文两遍

第一课　听写

1.	2.	3.	4.
5.	6.	7.	8.
9.	10.	11.	12.

第三课　听写

1.	2.	3.	4.
5.	6.	7.	8.
9.	10.	11.	12.

第五课　听写

1.	2.	3.	4.
5.	6.	7.	8.
9.	10.	11.	12.

第七课　听写

1.	2.	3.	4.
5.	6.	7.	8.
9.	10.	11.	12.

第九课　听写

1.	2.	3.	4.
5.	6.	7.	8.
9.	10.	11.	12.

1.	2.	3.	4.
5.	6.	7.	8.
9.	10.	11.	12.

1.	2.	3.	4.
5.	6.	7.	8.
9.	10.	11.	12.

1.	2.	3.	4.
5.	6.	7.	8.
9.	10.	11.	12.

第九课　听写

新双双中文教材 11

New Chinese Language and Culture Course

中国民俗与民间艺术
Chinese Folklore and Folk Art

练习本 双课

[美] 王双双 编著

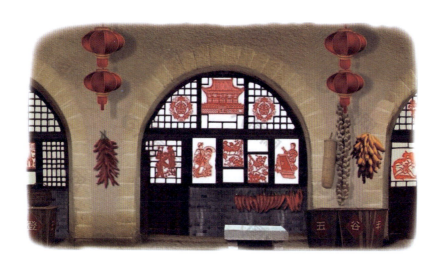

北京大学出版社

目　录

第二课　　喜庆的节日 …………………………………………… 1

第四课　　中国古建筑 …………………………………………… 7

第六课　　茶 ……………………………………………………… 12

第八课　　书法艺术 ……………………………………………… 18

第十课　　民间艺术——剪纸 …………………………………… 23

第二课 喜庆的节日

一 写生词

浓					
贴					
剪					
喜	庆				
挤	满				
气	氛				
习	俗				
团	聚				
饺	子				
除	夕				

聊	天				
亲	戚				
拜	年				
恭	喜				
吉	祥				
祝	福				
游	行				
富	裕				
鞭	炮				

二 下列汉字是由哪些部分组成的

团 → ☐ + ☐   贴 → ☐ + ☐

氛 → ☐ + ☐   吉 → ☐ + ☐

剪 → ☐ + ☐   炮 → ☐ + ☐

第二课 喜庆的节日

三 组词

喜庆　游行　团聚　祝贺

团 { _____ / _____ }　　庆 { _____ / _____ }

游 { _____ / _____ }　　祝 { _____ / _____ }

四 选字组词

（浓　农）民　　（亲　新）戚　　（饺　交）子

（浓　农）浓　　（亲　新）书　　（饺　交）给

五 写出反义词

淡　普通　悲伤　揭

喜庆—_____　　浓—_____

贴—_____　　独特—_____

第二课 喜庆的节日

六 给下面的词语加拼音

除夕 _____   聊天 _____   亲戚 _____

七 将方框中的词语与适当的解释连线

有钱没钱，吃饺子过年	春节拜年说的吉祥话。
一年不赶，赶三十晚	吃了饺子才算过年。
恭喜发财	中国农历新年。
春节	一定要春节前赶回家。
除夕之夜	春节的前一天晚上。

八 选择填空

1. 春节前火车站、飞机场都_____了回家的人潮。

2. 树上挂着一_____红灯笼。

3. 除夕之夜全家人围坐在一起吃_____。

4. 过了除夕是大年初一，人们走亲戚、看朋友，相互_____。

第二课 喜庆的节日

5. 孩子们放烟花和＿＿＿＿＿＿，看舞龙舞狮的游行表演。

6. 除夕晚上，家人一起＿＿＿＿说笑，看电视里的春晚节目。

九 根据课文判断对错

1. 春节是中国人心中最重要的节日。　　　　　　　　　　＿＿对＿＿错

2. 春节在中国农历的正月初一。　　　　　　　　　　　　＿＿对＿＿错

3. 春节是一年一次的全家大团圆。　　　　　　　　　　　＿＿对＿＿错

4. 老人给孩子拜年，会拿到一个红包。　　　　　　　　　＿＿对＿＿错

5. 春节孩子们穿新衣，放烟花和爆竹，看舞龙舞狮表演等。

　　　　　　　　　　　　　　　　　　　　　　　　　　＿＿对＿＿错

十 填写一副春联

新年大吉

年年如意春

岁岁平安日

十一 造句

聊天＿＿＿＿＿＿＿＿＿＿＿＿＿＿＿＿＿＿＿

第二课
喜庆的节日

十二 看图写出春节的主要活动,看看还少了一样,是什么?

1. 　　　　　　 2. 　　　　　　 3. 　　　　　　 4. 　　　　　　

5. 上面的春节主要习俗少了一样,想想是什么?请画出来

第二课 喜庆的节日

十三 阅读作业
选词语填表

农历正月初一
农历正月十五
农历五月初五
农历八月十五

贴春联　挂红灯
穿新衣　拜年　红包
舞龙舞狮　放鞭炮
　　　　吃饺子
赏花灯　吃元宵
赛龙船　吃粽子
家人团聚　赏月
　　　　吃月饼

节日名称	时间	节日活动
春节		
元宵节		
端午节		
中秋节		

十四 手工：做一张春节卡

十五 熟读课文两遍

第四课 中国古建筑

一 写生词

叠					
托					
檐					
吨					
寺	庙				
斗	拱				
构	件				
矩	形				
榫	卯				
勾	连				
荣	誉				

稳	固				
庄	严				
微	翘				
系	统				
测	绘				
顿	时				
白	描				
湮	没				
紫	禁	城			
金	碧	辉	煌		

二 下列汉字是由哪些部分组成的

第四课 中国古建筑

固 → □ + □   碧 → □ + □ + □

三 组词

结构　关系　牢固　金融

系 { _____　　　　融 { _____

构 { _____　　　　固 { _____

四 选字组词

结（构　沟）　　斗（拱　供）　　（矩　巨）型

水（构　沟）　　提（拱　供）　　（矩　巨）大

五 写出反义词

很久　直线　粗俗

曲线—_____　　顿时—_____　　优雅—_____

第四课 中国古建筑

六 将方框中的词语与适当的解释连线

湮没	开拓新领域、建设新事物的第一人。
紫禁城	随时间的流逝被埋没。
矩形	长方形。
台基	北京故宫原来的名字。
开创者	建筑的基础。

七 给下面的字加拼音，再组词

吨 _____ _____   顿 _____ _____

八 选择填空

斗拱　榫卯　湮没　抗震　系统　荣誉

1. 中国古代木结构建筑，构件之间直接用_____勾连。

2. 大屋顶靠木架_____托起。

3. 故宫是木结构的宫殿，所以_____能力很强。

4. 梁思成_____地考察了上千个古建筑。

5. 中国古建筑的大屋顶也在世界上赢得了_____。

6. 梁思成要追回那将要_____的古建筑艺术和技艺。

第四课
中国古建筑

九 根据课文判断对错

1. 木架结构和大屋顶是中国古建筑的特点。　　　　　　　___对___错

2. 斗拱是中国古建筑特有的结构，独有的构件。　　　　　___对___错

3. 木结构建筑抗震能力不强。　　　　　　　　　　　　　___对___错

4. 故宫是世界上最大、保存最好的木架结构建筑群。　　　___对___错

5. 梁思成考察中国古建筑，写了《中国建筑史》。　　　　___对___错

6. 梁思成用一生保护中国古建筑。　　　　　　　　　　　___对___错

十 造句

顿时＿＿＿＿＿＿＿＿＿＿＿＿＿＿＿＿＿＿＿＿＿＿＿＿＿＿

不仅……还……＿＿＿＿＿＿＿＿＿＿＿＿＿＿＿＿＿＿＿＿

十一 请将下图中的所有的"斗、坐斗"涂上红色

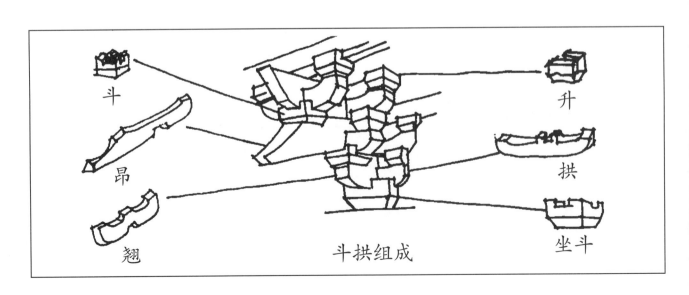

第四课 中国古建筑

十二 写一个你看到的中国古建筑

提示：长城　故宫　颐和园　天坛　孔庙等

① 古建筑的名字和建筑时间

② 描述古建筑：式样、颜色、装饰

③ 古建筑给你留下印象最深的是什么

十三 熟读课文两遍

第六课 茶

一 写生词

柴					
醋					
杯					
爽					
橙					
饮	料				
专	家				
划	破				
叮	咬				

红	肿				
生	疮				
发	酵				
红	艳				
销	售				
讲	究				
上	吐	下	泻		

二 下列汉字是由哪些部分组成的

柴 ⟶ ☐ + ☐   料 ⟶ ☐ + ☐

肿 ⟶ ☐ + ☐   艳 ⟶ ☐ + ☐

橙 ⟶ ☐ + ☐

第六课 茶

三 组词   　　　　　　　　　　　　　　划船　酱油　饮食　售货员

酱 { ____ / ____ }   　　　　　划 { ____ / ____ }

售 { ____ / ____ }   　　　　　饮 { ____ / ____ }

四 选字组词

将（油　来）　　专（家　说）　　岛（屿　烂）

酱（油　来）　　传（计　说）　　捣（屿　烂）

五 写出反义词   　　　　　　　　　　　　　　暗淡　随便

讲究——_____　　　　明亮——_____

第六课 茶

六 将方框中的词语与适当的解释连线

故乡	形容人神志清爽，心情舒畅。
神清气爽	出生或长期生活的地方。
至爱	最爱的。
茶之为饮，发乎神农氏	是神农发现茶叶能喝。

七 给下面的词语加拼音

专家 _____ 传说 _____ 转车 _____

八 选择填空

1. 中国有句话说："开门七件事——柴米油盐_____醋茶。"

2. 中国有朋友来了端一_____清茶。

3. 《茶经》上说："茶之为饮，发乎_____"。

4. 在中国云南、安徽、浙江、福建等省都有大片_____。

5. 根据不同的_____方法，形成了不同种类的茶。

第六课 茶

6. 中国人喝茶有三千年历史了。最早，茶为_____。

九 根据课文判断对错

1. 中国是茶叶的故乡。　　　　　　　　　　　　　___对___错

2. 中国俗话说："开门八件事——柴米油盐酱醋
   茶酒。"　　　　　　　　　　　　　　　　　　___对___错

3. 《茶经》说："茶之为饮，发乎神农氏。"　　　___对___错

4. 唐朝陆羽写了一本介绍茶叶的书叫《茶经》。　___对___错

5. 乌龙茶是半发酵茶。　　　　　　　　　　　　___对___错

6. 谈到喝茶，水很重要，山泉水最好。　　　　　___对___错

十 造句

讲究 _____

销售 _____

第六课 茶

十一　将下列各种茶叶与所属的茶叶种类连线

绿茶　　红茶　　乌龙茶　　黑茶　　花茶

西湖龙井　　大红袍　　茉莉花茶　　普洱茶　　祁门红茶

十二　阅读作业

选择回答：内蒙古草原、青藏高原的牧民，每天离不开茶。

原因是＿＿＿＿＿＿＿＿＿＿＿＿＿＿＿＿＿＿＿＿＿＿＿＿＿＿

＿＿＿＿＿＿＿＿＿＿＿＿＿＿＿＿＿＿＿＿＿＿＿＿＿＿＿＿＿

A. 茶帮助消化，补充维生素和微量元素，对健康有好处。

B. 茶比酒更容易买到。

十三　熟读课文两遍

第六课 茶

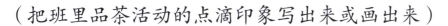

十四 品茶作业：写一篇随笔《我们品茶了》

（把班里品茶活动的点滴印象写出来或画出来）

提示：① 你看到的茶具是什么样子的

② 你品尝了几种茶，茶汤的气味、颜色、味道和其他印象等

③ 你生活中有关茶的小知识和故事，如茶叶蛋、珍珠奶茶的做法等

第六课									

第八课 书法艺术

一 写生词

匾	额				
匀	称				
墨	汁				
宣	纸				
虚	实				
抽	象				
意	境				
凭	空				
宛	然				

审	美				
布	局				
隶	书				
楷	书				
名	牌				
砚	台				
无	影	无	踪		

二 下列汉字是由哪些部分组成的

额 → ☐ + ☐   墨 → ☐ + ☐

砚 → ☐ + ☐   凭 → ☐ + ☐

第八课 书法艺术

三 组词

法律　棉布　额头　门牌

布 { _____
　　 _____

律 { _____
　　 _____

牌 { _____
　　 _____

额 { _____
　　 _____

四 选字组词

一（遍　匾）　　（墨　黑）汁　　（凭　任）空

牌（遍　匾）　　（墨　黑）夜　　（凭　任）务

五 写出反义词

四周　具体

中央—_____　　　　抽象—_____

六 给下面的词语加拼音

楷书 _____　　　　隶书 _____

凭空 _____　　　　匾额 _____

第八课 书法艺术

七 将方框里的词语和适当的解释连线

无影无踪	把别人的注意力引到自己这方面来。
端正	形容完全消失，不知去向。
吸引	物体不歪斜，各部分保持平衡。
宛然	仿佛，很像。

八 选择填空

1. 故宫精美的书法作品＿＿＿＿＿＿着游客的目光。

2. 汉字从诞生之日起，就有了自己的＿＿＿＿＿＿要求。

3. 在整篇书法作品中要讲究整体＿＿＿＿＿＿。

4. 文房四宝是：笔、墨、纸、＿＿＿＿＿＿。

5. 美丽的瓦当＿＿＿＿＿＿建筑物。

九 根据课文判断对错

1. 参观故宫会看到许多精美的书法作品。　　　＿＿对＿＿错

2. 用毛笔写好汉字并不容易。　　　＿＿对＿＿错

第八课
书法艺术

3. 常见的书法字体有：隶书、楷书、行书等。　　　___对___错

4. 现在我们常用的是楷书和行书。　　　　　　　　___对___错

5. 书法作品在中国只是艺术品。　　　　　　　　　___对___错

6. 中国钱币上的字都讲究书法的艺术性。　　　　　___对___错

十　造句

除了……之外 _____

名牌 _____

十一　下列四个字，选出你最喜欢的一个写出来

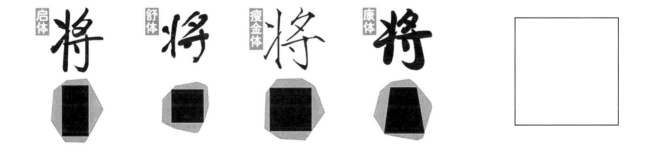

第八课
书法艺术

十二 照着篆字帖、楷体帖写字

千 文
天 地
宇 宙
玄 黄
洪 荒
日 月
盈 昃

天下皆知美之
为美斯恶已皆
知善之为善斯
不善已故有无

第十课 民间艺术——剪纸

☆ ---------- ☆ ---------- ☆

一 写生词

糊					
剪	纸				
来	临				
装	饰				
单	调				
平	凡				
图	案				
熟	练				
艺	人				

魔	术				
纯	朴				
五	谷	丰	登		
心	灵	手	巧		
乡	土	气	息		

二 组词

调皮　一叠纸　剪刀　临走

剪 {　　　　　}　　　调 {　　　　　}

临 {　　　　　}　　　叠 {　　　　　}

第十课 民间艺术——剪纸

三 选字组词

（详 祥）细　　　（前 剪）纸　　　（遗 贵）产

吉（详 祥）　　　（前 剪）后　　　（遗 贵）重

四 写出反义词

丰富　离开

来临—_____　　　单调—_____

五 给下面的字词加拼音

吉祥 _____　　魔术 _____　　叠 _____

六 找出剪纸中的吉祥字和吉祥语，并写出

_____

_____

第十课 民间艺术——剪纸

七 将方框里的词语与适当的解释连线

五谷丰登	粮食丰收。
吉祥如意	祝贺人发财富裕的话。
恭喜发财	不能作为凭证或根据。
不足为凭	祝他人美满称心。

八 选择填空

1. 别看这小小的剪纸，它轻快地＿＿＿＿＿＿着百姓的生活。

2. 古时中国农村房屋的窗户上糊着白纸，很＿＿＿＿＿＿。

3. 窗花贴在窗户上，＿＿＿＿＿＿平凡的窗户就有了生气。

4. 人们认为剪花好的女人＿＿＿＿＿＿手巧。

5. 中国剪纸的图案，带有浓重的＿＿＿＿＿＿气息。

6. 目前中国剪纸已被列入世界文化＿＿＿＿＿＿。

第十课 民间艺术——剪纸

九 根据课文判断对错

1. 剪纸是中国的一种民间艺术。　　　　　　　　　___对___错

2. 中国剪纸大约有1,500多年的历史了。　　　　　___对___错

3. 中国人结婚时会在窗上贴"红双喜"剪纸。　　　___对___错

4. 剪纸只有单色的，没有彩色的。　　　　　　　　___对___错

5. 过去在农村，每个女孩子都学习剪纸。　　　　　___对___错

6. 过春节贴剪纸，带给人们浓浓的喜庆气氛。　　　___对___错

十 造句

来临 _____

顿时 _____

第十课 民间艺术——剪纸

十一 阅读作业选词填空

> 剪刀 绣花 唐宋 好纸 刻刀 精致 戏曲人物 浓艳

1. 扬州在中国江苏省。早在_____时期，扬州就有剪纸报春的习俗。扬州的剪纸艺术，离不开扬州的_____。扬州也是丝绸之乡，百姓服饰以_____为美，而绣花时要用剪纸为底样。由此，扬州剪纸便从刺绣花样中走了出来。扬州剪纸多为一色，线条_____流畅。

2. 河北蔚县剪纸是用_____"刻"出来的。剪纸内容还有_____。蔚县剪纸有彩色的，而且色彩_____鲜明。

十二 用红纸剪出"春"或"福"字

提示：① 平面春字：将方纸对折，画出图样再剪

② 立体春字：将方纸对角折三次，画出图样再剪

十三 熟读课文两遍

第二课　听写

1.	2.	3.	4.
5.	6.	7.	8.
9.	10.	11.	12.

第四课　听写

1.	2.	3.	4.
5.	6.	7.	8.
9.	10.	11.	12.

第六课　听写

1.	2.	3.	4.
5.	6.	7.	8.
9.	10.	11.	12.

第八课　听写

1.	2.	3.	4.
5.	6.	7.	8.
9.	10.	11.	12.

第十课　听写

1.	2.	3.	4.
5.	6.	7.	8.
9.	10.	11.	12.

1.	2.	3.	4.
5.	6.	7.	8.
9.	10.	11.	12.

1.	2.	3.	4.
5.	6.	7.	8.
9.	10.	11.	12.

1.	2.	3.	4.
5.	6.	7.	8.
9.	10.	11.	12.